Healthcare Solved

Healthcare Solved

–Real Answers, No Politics

Debra A. Smith DO, MIHM, MBA,
FACPM, FAOCOPM, FAIHQ

2009

Global Health Press · Indianapolis

Published by Global Health Press, PO Box 40443, Indianapolis, IN 46240-
0443 USA.

First Edition

Smith, Debra A., 1967-

ISBN: 978-0-557-09032-7

Table of Contents

Introduction

This book is written to provide the public with a real solution to the escalating cost of healthcare. If you are looking for a textbook on the history of healthcare in the United States, look elsewhere. This book analyzes the current situation and puts forth practical answers for containing costs while improving the quality of service to all. Inside you will find the evidence base to support the rationale used. It is not a political manifesto, but it is written in response to politicians attempting to hijack healthcare for their own gain at the expense of the American people. As both a physician and economist, I believe I have a more complete picture than most purported experts on how healthcare is *actually* delivered and where the money is really going. The answers will likely surprise you. However, if we are going to have a serious debate about healthcare, it is time for America's people, employers and healthcare professionals to fully understand and reclaim this most important issue.

Note: This book is heavily documented as there are too many in this supposed debate who are spouting off answers and statistics which are naive, uninformed, inaccurate or downright lies. Any italics, bolding or font changes in quotations are mine for emphasis. Also, I have used the generic male tense when referring to doctors, patients, etc. This is in no way a slight to the accomplished female gender, it is merely a convention to avoid the awkward s/he or using the plural "they" when referring to a singular person.

Chapter 1

Where is all the money going?

Medical costs are spiraling out of control. Health costs increased 9.9% last year alone.[1] More and more health insurers are losing money, being downgraded in the market, bought out and/or consolidated.[2,3] This trend is not just the result of investment losses due to the latest financial crisis, but losses due to underwriting.

> Health insurers including **Humana**(HUM:NYSE), **UnitedHealth Group**(UNH:NYSE) and **WellCare Health Plans**(WCG:NYSE) reported combined third-quarter earnings of $2.6 billion, setting up what will probably be the weakest year since 2003…according to the National Association of Insurance Commissioners' health financial statement. Thirty percent of health insurers recorded net losses.
>
> Health insurers have two main sources of income: underwriting, the difference between premiums and the amount paid out in claims;

---

[1] Of this, 3.7% is due to medical inflation (annual medical CPI); the rest of the increase is due to expanding demand for medical goods and services and advancements in new medical technology and drugs.

[2] *HMO stocks fall as Aetna, UnitedHealth downgraded*. Reuters. July 3, 2008. http://www.reuters.com/article/hotStocksNews/idUSN0336314420080703

[3] *A.M. Best Completes Review of Health Insurer Public Data Ratings*. BUSINESS WIRE: Thompson Business Intelligence Service. November 25, 2008. http://www.insurancenewsnet.com/article.asp?a=top_news&neID=20081125290.2_2161009c e3f58f95

and investment income...Health-insurance companies recorded $6.5 billion in investment income during 2007, equal to 40% of profits. Based on trends, total investment income for 2008 may be about $3.4 billion, a decline of 48% [due to the decline in interest rates]. In the third quarter, investment income tumbled 46% to $527 million from the same period a year earlier...Still, 70% of insurers that posted investment losses had positive net income, including subsidiaries of **Coventry Health Care**(CVH:NYSE) and **Wellpoint**(WLP:NYSE).

Investment losses weren't the cause of insurers losing money in the first nine months of 2008. However, that substantial income helps keep premiums down and companies more competitive. Health-insurance companies make most of their profits on underwriting income. Insurers made $9.7 billion from underwriting in 2007, a slim 2.4% margin.

...In previous quarters [of 2008], medical expenses had been rising faster than premiums... Thirty-six percent of insurers recorded underwriting losses in the first nine months of the year, up 18%, or $200 million, to $1.3 billion. Three-quarters of companies that lost money on underwriting also recorded an overall net loss. Thirty-six insurers had underwriting losses that exceeded $10 million, including subsidiaries of **Centene** (CNC:NYSE), Humana, **Molina Healthcare** (MOH:NYSE), UnitedHealth Group and WellCare Health Plans.[4]

If private insurers are operating with only a 2.4% margin, it seems highly unlikely that government–run health plan will break even, *let alone do a better job* of managing costs on its own.

An aging population is further increasing the demands on an already strained system. While the debate as to whether healthcare is a right is yet to be settled, both physicians and their patients expect that they should be able to provide or receive, as the case may be, the best healthcare possible regardless of cost. Morally and ethically, the

[4] *Health Insurers Profits Sink.* Gavin Magor, TheStreet.com Ratings Senior Health Insurance Analyst. March 26, 2009. http://www.thestreet.com/story/10477877/1/health-insurers-profits-sink.html

standard should be to provide patients the best healthcare; however, financial realities quickly set in when the hospital bill arrives and a family's lifetime savings are wiped out.

We have also sought to prevent disease by educating our patients about the consequences of their lifestyle choices. But, the effects of wellness and prevention often take years or even decades to evaluate for results. At the risk of being called a heretic by my colleagues in public health, prevention will not have any immediate impact on healthcare costs.

Consider this—It was not until 1965 that Congress required all cigarette packages distributed in the United States to carry a health warning.[5] This was done in response to the report entitled, *Smoking and Health: Report of the Advisory Committee to the Surgeon General,* which was issued a year earlier.

After the Surgeon General's report was issued, the prevalence of smoking in this country began to decline from its 1965 high of 42.4% (51.9% of men, 33.9% of women).[6] Despite more than 40 years of public service announcements, campaigns to stop smoking, government-sponsored quit lines, etc., about one in five Americans *still* smokes.[7] According to the National Cancer Institute, U.S. National Institutes of Health (NIH), smoking is the cause of 87% of

[5] *The Reports of the Surgeon General: The 1964 Report on Smoking and Health.* Profiles in Science: National Library of Medicine Web site
http://profiles.nlm.nih.gov/NN/Views/Exhibit/narrative/smoking.html [Accessed 6/20/09]
[6] CDC. MMWR: *Tobacco Use Among Adults--US, 2005.* Vol. 55(42):1145-1148, 10/27/06. National Center for Health Statistics. National Health Interview Survey 1965-2005.
[7] Thorne SL, Malarcher A, Maurice E, Caraballo R. *Cigarette Smoking Among Adults --- United States, 2007.* Morbidity & Mortality Weekly Report, CDC; Vol. 57(45);1221-1226, 11/14/08.
http://www.cdc.gov/mmwr/preview/mmwrhtml/mm5745a2.htm

all deaths due to lung cancer.[8] Since the effects of smoking linger even decades after a person quits their habit, it was not until 1992 that we began to see a decline in the incidence rates of cancer of the lung and bronchus by year, race and sex.[9]

Emphasizing preventive testing and good health habits saves money and preserves health in the very long run. However, in the short and intermediate run, they have been shown to cost the system more money.

There is the mistaken notion that because something is cost-effective, it is cost saving. While this may be true when comparing treatments for a disease, it is *seldom* true with prevention. If a treatment is found to be the most cost-effective, you are getting the most value for your money. Prevention and early detection involves education and testing of the entire *potentially affected, asymptomatic* population in order to prevent or detect a case of the disease. This means society spends money on the education, testing and follow-up for all potential victims of disease. But, the benefits of those efforts, both clinical and financial, are only realized by those who eventually would have developed the disease.[10] *The goal of prevention is primarily to prevent morbidity, suffering, and mortality, death, rather than to save money.*

Consider even one of the most cost-effective prevention methods,

---

[8] Cigarette Smoking: Questions & Answers. National Cancer Institute: National Institutes of Health Web site http://www.cancer.gov/cancertopics/factsheet/Tobacco/cancer [Accessed 6/20/09]
[9] *Cancer of Lung and Bronchus*. SEER Cancer Statistics Review 1975-2006; National Cancer Institute http://seer.cancer.gov/csr/1975_2006/results_merged/sect_15_lung_bronchus.pdf
[10] Teutsch, S. *Cost-Effectiveness of Prevention*. Medscape 7/13/2006 http://www.medscape.com/viewarticle/540199 [Accessed 6/8/09]

breast cancer screening. "Similar to other cancer screening tests, the large majority (80 percent to 90 percent) of abnormal screening mammograms or clinical breast exams are false-positives. These may require follow-up testing or invasive procedures such as breast biopsy to resolve the diagnosis, and can result in anxiety, inconvenience, discomfort, and additional medical expenses…The proportion of false-positive results that lead to biopsy varies substantially in different settings."[11] Mammogram screening reduces deaths from breast cancer by less than 20%.[12] *While more screening does reduce morbidity and mortality, it costs money.*

In 2006 the National Commission on Prevention Priorities identified and ranked the most cost-effective and clinically disease burden reducing preventive services. These include screening and counseling for tobacco use and problem drinking; screening for colorectal cancer, breast cancer, and cervical cancer, Chlamydia in young women, cholesterol, hypertension, and vision problems; discussing aspirin use with high-risk adults; and immunizing children against childhood illnesses, immunizing adults with the influenza vaccine and immunizing the elderly against pneumococcal disease.[13]

With rare exceptions, such as immunizations, prevention does not actually save any money, but it does provide a potentially good value

[11] *U.S. Preventive Services Task Force (USPSTF) Screening for Breast Cancer Recommendations and Rationale.* Agency for Healthcare Quality Research Web site [Accessed 6/30/09] http://www.ahrq.gov/clinic/3rduspstf/breastcancer/brcanrr.htm
[12] Ibid.
[13] Maciosek MV, Coffield AB, Edwards NM, Flottemesch TJ, Goodman MJ, Solberg LI. *Priorities Among Effective Clinical Preventive Services: Results of a Systematic Review and Analysis.* American Journal of Preventive Medicine, Vol 31 (1), Pages 52-6. http://download.journals.elsevierhealth.com/pdfs/journals/0749-3797/PIIS0749379706001243.pdf

for society. However, identifying a potential problem is a waste of resources if you cannot affect change.

Getting patients to change their life patterns is extraordinarily challenging, whether it involves smoking, drinking, eating or exercise habits. Success rates are low, which is why many physicians have given up on encouraging lifestyle changes. Additionally, the cumulative effects of our bad habits and chronic diseases, be it smoking, obesity, hypercholesterolemia, etc., tend to progress silently for years, if not decades, before becoming symptomatic and creating any serious motivation for change. *The problem with using prevention alone to lower the burden of disease in the population is that we do not have the more than 25 years needed to see significant results. We need to cut costs now!*

Economists consider healthcare a "normal good," meaning that spending is directly correlated with income. As our income rises, we demand more and better health care. In essence, wealth determines spending on healthcare. The usual economic principle of *diminishing marginal utility* does not seem to apply to healthcare. The marginal utility or satisfaction of each additional purchase of an item or service does not produce a diminishing marginal return. (My economics professor described the concept of diminishing marginal returns like this: If you go to a picnic and start eating hot dogs, one is good. Two is also good, maybe better because you did not wolf it down in your hunger, but actually enjoyed it. But as you continue to eat them, each additional hot dog is less and less enjoyable.) Healthcare does not follow this rule. More is perceived as better, up to the point that any additional benefit received is considered an inconvenience by the consumer patient.

Therefore, when coverage levels are increased, whether by a company benefit plan or government program, so too are total healthcare costs. The heart of the issue is that the healthcare consumer is not the same person who is paying the bill. This is the reason insurance co-payments came about.

Given this fact, it would be foolish to think that universal coverage, whether privately or publically paid, would lower total expenditures in this country, in the present environment. True healthcare reform requires much more, as you will see in coming chapters.

Chapter 2

Why not use the Medicare model for the nation's healthcare?

This solution has been proposed by many well-meaning people lobbying for universal care. It seems our older folks have a decent system for receiving care. There does not appear to be any of the dreaded rationing that so many fear. Medicare Supplemental (MedSup) plans exist for those who want additional coverage, and there are about a dozen or so options from which to choose. For the most part, people can go to the doctor of their choice, unless of course they purchase an HMO MedSup plan which requires them to use physicians in their panel. There is even a prescription drug benefit now.

It has been working quite well for the last 44 years.[14] Why can't we expand it to cover all of our uninsured?

In 1965 when the Medicare program was created, the population demographics were quite different than they are today. We know birth rates began to decline in the 1960s with the advent of "the pill." If you

---

[14] Centers for Medicare & Medicaid Services Web site http://www.cms.hhs.gov/History/ [Accessed 6/20/09]

were 65 years old in 1965, your average life expectancy was 14.8 more years[15] as opposed to 18.7 years[16] today. In short, life expectancy has increased four years for those over 65. The largest segment of the population then and now were the baby boomers. Let's follow this cohort (group of individuals) through time.

Take a look at the population pyramid in 1965. It shows the number of people, in millions, by sex in each age group.

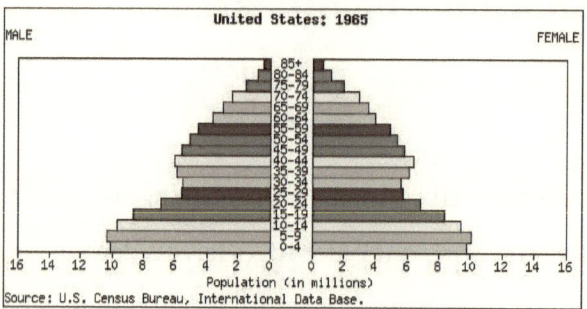

There were approximately 194 million people. The average age was 28, and 9.5% of the population was over the age of 65, according to the U.S. Census Bureau. Notice that the largest age groups are those under 20 years old; these are the baby boomers.

Now look at today's population pyramid. There are now approximately 307 million people in the country. The average age is 37, and 12.9% of the population is over 65.

[15] Bell F, Miller M. *Unisex life expectancies at birth and at age 65*. Actuarial Note; Number 2004.2; September 2004
Social Security Administration, Office of the Chief Actuary, Baltimore, Maryland
http://www.ssa.gov/OACT/NOTES/ran2/an2004-2.pdf
[16] *Table 101: Average Number of Years of Life Remaining by Sex and Age: 1989 to 2005*. US Census Bureau.
http://www.census.gov/compendia/statab/tables/09s0101.pdf

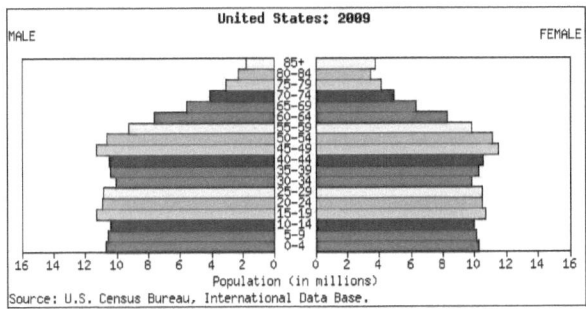

Look at the age group over 45 and you will again see the baby boomer bulge. Those age 15 to 30 are generally the "boomlets"— children of the boomers. Unlike their fruitful WWII generation parents, the boomers have just about replaced themselves in numbers when they had children.

In 2019, just 10 years from now, the population is projected to be 338 million with an average age of 38. The over 65 age group will likely comprise 16% of the population.

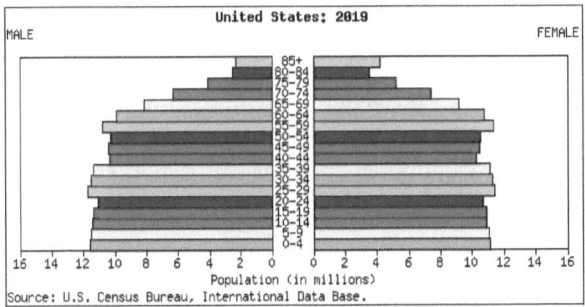

In 20 years, the population is projected to be 370 million. The average age will likely be 38, and 19.1% of the population will be over 65.

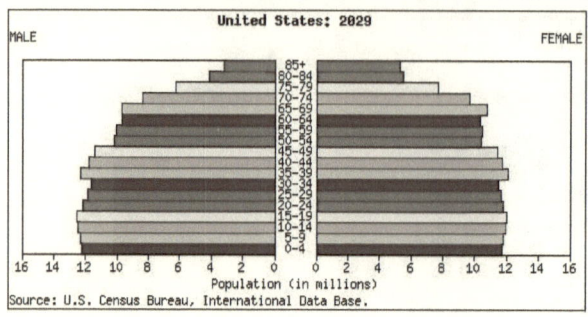

Compounding the problem, we will have doubled the percentage of people receiving benefits in the population since the program was designed, and they will be receiving benefits longer.

Mr. Richard W. Fisher is president and CEO of the Federal Reserve Bank of Dallas and a member of the Federal Open Market Committee, the Federal Reserve's principal group for setting monetary policymaking. He laid out the problem eloquently in an address to the Commonwealth Club of California on May 28, 2008:

> In the distance, I see a frightful storm brewing in the form of untethered government debt…Unless we take steps to deal with it, the long-term fiscal situation of the federal government will be unimaginably more devastating to our economic prosperity than the subprime debacle and the recent debauching of credit markets that we are now working so hard to correct.

> …Medicare was a pay-as-you-go program from the very beginning…Please sit tight while I walk you through the math of Medicare. As you may know, the program comes in three parts: Medicare Part A, which covers hospital stays; Medicare B, which covers doctor visits; and Medicare D, the drug benefit that went into effect just 29 months ago. The infinite-horizon present discounted value of the unfunded liability for Medicare A is $34.4 trillion. The unfunded liability of Medicare B is an additional $34 trillion. The shortfall for Medicare D adds another $17.2 trillion. The total? *If you wanted to cover the unfunded liability of all three programs*

today, you would be stuck with an $85.6 trillion bill. That is more than six times as large as the bill for Social Security. It is more than six times the annual output of the entire U.S. economy.

Why is the Medicare figure so large? There is a mix of reasons, really. In part, it is due to the same birthrate and life-expectancy issues that affect Social Security. In part, it is due to ever-costlier advances in medical technology and the willingness of Medicare to pay for them. And in part, it is due to expanded benefits—the new drug benefit program's unfunded liability is by itself one-third greater than all of Social Security's.

Add together the unfunded liabilities from Medicare and Social Security, and it comes to $99.2 trillion over the infinite horizon. Traditional Medicare composes about 69 percent, the new drug benefit roughly 17 percent and Social Security the remaining 14 percent.

I want to remind you that I am only talking about the *unfunded* portions of Social Security and Medicare. **It is what the current payment scheme of Social Security payroll taxes, Medicare payroll taxes, membership fees for Medicare B, copays, deductibles and all other revenue currently channeled to our entitlement system will not cover under current rules.** These existing revenue streams must remain in place in perpetuity to handle the "funded" entitlement liabilities. Reduce or eliminate this income and the unfunded liability grows. Increase benefits and the liability grows as well.

Let's say…every U.S. citizen who is alive today decided to fully address this unfunded liability through lump-sum payments from our own pocketbooks, so that all of us and all future generations could be secure in the knowledge that we and they would receive promised benefits in perpetuity. How much would we have to pay if we split the tab? Again, the math is painful. With a total population of 304 million, from infants to the elderly, the per-person payment to the federal treasury would come to $330,000. This comes to $1.3 million per family of four—over 25 times the average household's income.

Clearly, once-and-for-all contributions would be an unbearable burden. Alternatively, we could address the entitlement shortfall through policy changes that would affect ourselves and future generations. For example, a permanent 68 percent increase in federal income tax revenue—from individual and corporate taxpayers—would suffice to fully fund our entitlement programs. Or we could instead divert 68 percent of current income-tax revenues from their intended uses to the entitlement system, which would accomplish the same thing.

Suppose we decided to tackle the issue solely on the spending side. It turns out that total discretionary spending in the federal budget, if maintained at its current share of GDP in perpetuity, is 3 percent larger than the entitlement shortfall. So all we would have to do to fully fund our nation's entitlement programs would be to cut discretionary spending by 97 percent. But hold on. That discretionary spending includes defense and national security, education, the environment and many other areas, not just those controversial earmarks that make the evening news. All of them would have to be cut—almost eliminated, really—to tackle this problem through discretionary spending.

I hope that gives you some idea of just how large the problem is. And just to drive an important point home, these spending cuts or tax increases would need to be made immediately and maintained in perpetuity to solve the entitlement deficit problem. Discretionary spending would have to be reduced by 97 percent not only for our generation, but for our children and their children and every generation of children to come. And similarly on the taxation side, income tax revenue would have to rise 68 percent and remain that high forever. Remember, though, I said tax *revenue*, not tax *rates*. Who knows how much individual and corporate tax rates would have to change to increase revenue by 68 percent?

If these possible solutions to the unfunded-liability problem seem draconian, it's because they are draconian. But they do serve to give you a sense of the severity of the problem. To be sure, there are ways to lessen the reliance on any single policy and the burden borne by any particular set of citizens. Most proposals to address long-term entitlement debt, for example, rely on a combination of tax increases, benefit reductions and eligibility changes to find the trillions necessary to safeguard the system over the long term.

No combination of tax hikes and spending cuts, though, will change the total burden borne by current and future generations. For the existing unfunded liabilities to be covered in the end, someone must pay $99.2 trillion more or receive $99.2 trillion less than they have been currently promised. This is a cold, hard fact. The decision we must make is whether to shoulder a substantial portion of that burden today or compel future generations to bear its full weight.

…It is only natural to cast about for a solution—any solution—to avoid the fiscal pain we know is necessary because we succumbed to complacency and put off dealing with this looming fiscal disaster. Throughout history, many nations, when confronted by sizable debts they were unable or unwilling to repay, have seized upon an apparently painless solution to this dilemma: monetization. Just have the monetary authority run cash off the printing presses until the debt is repaid, the story goes, then promise to be responsible from that point on and hope your sins will be forgiven by God and Milton Friedman and everyone else.

…The inflation that results from the flood of money into the economy turns out to be far worse than the fiscal pain those countries hoped to avoid.[17]

Fisher continued.

…The way we resolve these liabilities—and resolve them we must—will affect our own well-being as well as the prospects of future generations and the global economy. Failing to face up to our responsibility will produce the mother of all financial storms. The warning signals have been flashing for years, but we find it easier to ignore them than to take action. Will we take the painful fiscal steps necessary to prevent the storm by reducing and eventually eliminating our fiscal imbalances? That depends on you.

I mean "you" literally. This situation is of your own creation. When you berate your representatives or senators or presidents for the mess we are in, you are really berating yourself. You elect them. You are the ones who let them get away with burdening your children and grandchildren rather than yourselves with the bill for your entitlement programs.

[17] *Storms on the Horizon*. Presentation by Richard W. Fisher [Dallas Federal Reserve Bank President] Remarks before the Commonwealth Club of California, San Francisco, CA; May 28, 2008. http://www.dallasfed.org/news/speeches/fisher/2008/fs080528.cfm

This issue transcends political affiliation. When George Shultz, one of San Francisco's greatest Republican public servants, was director of President Nixon's Office of Management and Budget, he became worried about the amount of money Congress was proposing to spend. After some nights of tossing and turning, he called legendary staffer Sam Cohen into his office. Cohen had a long memory of budget matters and knew every zig and zag of budget history. "Sam," Shultz asked, "tell me something just between you and me. Is there any difference between Republicans and Democrats when it comes to spending money?" Cohen looked at him, furrowed his brow and, after thinking about it, replied, "Mr. Shultz, there is only one difference: Democrats enjoy it more."

…You have it in your power as the electors of our fiscal authorities to prevent this destruction. Please do so. [18]

According to the Government Accountability Office (GAO) audit report of the federal government's consolidated financial statements, *in 2008 Medicare hospital insurance benefits began to exceed program tax in their revenues.*[19] There is already more money going out than coming into the program.

As a matter of health policy, since the average life expectancy is now a good four years longer (and growing) than when the financial model for Medicare was developed, the age of eligibility should have been increased at intervals along the way. It *already* should have been increased to 69. The reality is since people are living longer, they have more years to be productive. Indeed we need them to be productive longer and add to our nation's economic output, because there will be twice as many of them percentage-wise to support in

---

[18] Ibid.
[19] *A Citizen's Guide to the 2008 Financial Report of the U.S. Government: The Federal Government's Financial Health.* The Government Accountability Office, 2008. http://www.gao.gov/financial/citizensguide2008.pdf

their later years. Politically, there is probably not a politician with the intestinal fortitude to make such a suggestion since this age group is the most active voting block. Common sense would dictate that economics and epidemiology should prevail, but expectations and politics are another matter.

It would be a violation of the current Medicare contract to take on additional Medicare enrollees when we do not as yet have any concrete or foreseeable means of paying for the obligations we have *already* promised to those currently insured. In the private sector, any company doing this would be prohibited from doing business by state regulators. Why should the federal government be held to a lesser standard when it is proposing to offer such services to its citizens? Government does not have a right to be irresponsible. As Abraham Lincoln said, our nation has a "government of the people, by the people, for the people."[20] We, the people, must put our financial house in order to sustain, let alone expand, any government-provided health benefits. So let's begin.

[20] Lincoln's Gettysburg Address

Chapter 3

Follow the money[21]

The chief complaint about our healthcare system is that it's too costly, so let's begin to examine the roots of those costs. Less than 1% of the population accounts for 30% of the total medical costs,[22, 23] most of which are cancer patients. Another 11% of the population accounts for 43% of the costs,[24] most of these are patients with chronic diseases at advanced or end stages. As you can see, almost ¾ of all healthcare spending is from just 12% of the population. It is not the coronary artery disease or hypercholesterolemia diagnoses that are costly; it is the myocardial infarction (MI) that requires percutaneous transluminal coronary angioplasty (PTCA aka balloon angioplasty) or

---

[21] During the Watergate scandal, which unseated President Richard M. Nixon, Deep Throat told investigative reporters to "Follow the money."

[22] Forman SA, Kelliher M, Wood G. *Clinical Improvement with Bottom Line Impact: Custom Care Planning for Patients with Acute and Chronic Illnesses in a Managed Care Setting.* American Journal of Medical Management; 1997; 3(7), 1039-1048. http://www.ajmc.com/media/pdf/AJMC1997JulyForman1039_1048.pdf

[23] Cote, B. The Physician's Role in Securing Patient Access to Appropriate Therapies: Sharing the Stage with Patients and Payers: A review of a symposium held in conjunction with the American Society of Clinical Oncology (ASCO). Oncology Business Review; July 2008, p. 23-29. http://www.oncbiz.com/documents/OBR_july08_BI.pdf

[24] Ibid.

coronary artery bypass graft (CABG) surgery, the aortic aneurysm repair, the atrial fibrillation that requires a pacemaker. The money goes to treating the end results of these chronic diseases that often take decades to develop. That's why it takes so long to reap the benefits of prevention. As a clinician, I believe prevention is necessary, as is adequate continuing medical management. But, it's not the most effective way to impact healthcare expenditures now.

The insurance industry refers to these as catastrophic conditions and illnesses, also known as "shock" or "cat" claims. About 70 odd conditions fall into this category, including such things as transplants, cancers, cardiovascular diseases, immune diseases and joint replacements. Also included are low birth weight and premature babies, as well as multiple births related to the use of fertility drugs.

If you think about it, it should not be too surprising that this is where the money is being spent. If the costs of providing care for these catastrophic conditions could be better managed, the system would be significantly healthier. We must start the cost cutting now.

"We have the best healthcare in the world."

This is what our politicians and healthcare professionals would have you believe; they believe it themselves. We certainly pay more than enough for the best care. In fact, we have convinced many around the world we have the best. When I was working in the Third World, if Westerners had the choice between a German, French, British or American doctor, they would almost invariably choose the American doctor, regardless of their own nationality. While American medicine seems to have the best public relations, the best healthcare is another matter.

In reality, the United States ranks 1st in costliness and 1st in trauma care, but 37th in overall health system performance, according to the World Health Organization's 2000 Annual Report.[25] Life expectancy in the United States ranked 28th in the world. Obviously, there is room for improvement. Upon closer examination, it is other First World countries that would appear to have some advantage. Given the worldwide availability of and access to medical literature through such resources as Medline and PubMed[26], etc., one would think that medicine is practiced similarly across the First World, or is it? Do some countries have a competitive advantage over others in treating certain disease?

A.T. Still MD, DO, founder of the osteopathic medical profession,[27] said that it was the physician's job to "find health." Keeping in mind "...those who are strong and well have no need of a physician, but those who are weak and sick..."[28] we have to triage, prioritize, where and how we focus our attention. We need to make an immediate impact on costs. If we are going to find health for our healthcare system, we need to start with the high cost endpoints of

---

[25] World Health Report 2000 - Annex Table 2 Basic Indicators for all Member States. World Health Organization, 2000.
http://www.who.int/whr2001/2001/archives/2000/en/pdf/AnnexTable02.pdf
[26] This is a search engine for all peer-reviewed medical literature published around the world; these are credible journals which have experts in the field review the study before it is published. This search engine is maintained by the US National Institutes of Health's, National Library of Medicine.
[27] There are over 60,000 osteopathic physicians in the Untied States in all specialties and sub-specialties of medicine. In the US, osteopathic physicians (DOs) have similar training, the same practice rights and professional obligations as their allopathic (MD) counterparts as recognized by the federal government and in all fifty states.
[28] Mark 2:17 Bible

disease, rather than the starting points.

Let's begin our search for health by examining how various conditions are treated.

For certain treatments and procedures, such as a knee replacement in an otherwise healthy person, the comparative costs are similar across the First World, when standardized for inflation, currencies and healthcare system discounts. This should not be surprising, given that there are only a few companies in the world that make the prosthetics and the preoperative and postoperative care is fairly standardized.

For other conditions, such as kidney transplants, the comparative cost analysis does not bear out a similar result. In fact, certain countries appear to have a *competitive advantage* in treating certain diseases. Clinical evidence suggests that this exists across a spectrum of catastrophic conditions.[29,30] *This phenomenon also appears to bear out financially, even when standardized for the discounts of the various healthcare systems.* When these results are then clinically analyzed, one will find that these countries are doing something different in the care and follow-up of these patients that makes them significantly more cost-effective in providing treatment.

Belgium is one example. In a study published in July 2005, Chaib-Eddour, et. al.,[31] reported the average first-year costs for a kidney

---

[29] Payer, Lynn. Medicine & Culture: Varieties of Treatment in the United States, England, West Germany, and France. New York: Henry Holt and Company, 1988.

[30] Hussey PS, Anderson GF, Osborn R, Feek C, McLaughlin V, Millar J, Epstein A. *How Does The Quality Of Care Compare In Five Countries?* Health Affairs, May/June 2004; 23(3): 89-99.
http://content.healthaffairs.org/cgi/reprint/23/3/89?maxtoshow=&HITS=80&hits=80&RESULTFORMAT=&andorexacttitle=and&andorexacttitleabs=and&andorexactfulltext=and&searchid=1&FIRSTINDEX=160&sortspec=relevance&fdate=1/1/2004&tdate=12/31/2004&resourcetype=HWCIT

[31] Chaib-Eddour D, Chaib-Eddour H, Malaise J, Mourad M, Squifflet JP. *Cost of Renal*

transplant as €39,827. The study collected one year of cost data and was published in July of 2005. Presumably, the costs were collected over the preceding year or two. (The article did not state if costs were standardized to the year of publication, which is somewhat problematic.) Let's assume cost data was collected from January 1, 2004 through March 1, 2005. The average exchange rate during that period was 1€ to $1.2529. [32] Thus a kidney transplant in Belgium costs $49,899. The Belgian healthcare system operates at a 48% discount to ours. In other words, its expenditures are 52% of ours.[33] Costing up to the US system, the average cost of a kidney transplant would be $95,352. Yet this is considerably less than the average US claims paid from that period, which was about $127,357.[34] It seems the Belgians were likely doing something different in their clinical care that resulted in a savings of $32,005.

Until now, there have been limitations on such comparative studies. Cost analysis and cost-effectiveness research in medicine is yet in its infancy, and standards for peer-review, which assures useful, meaningful information, have not been well-established. In general, the studies tend to be poorly constructed, with major gaps in their collection of data, analyses or in the meaningful reporting of data.

Transplant in Belgium. Transplantation Proceedings, 37, 2819-2820 (2005). http://download.journals.elsevierhealth.com/pdfs/journals/0041-1345/PIIS0041134505005749.pdf
[32] Oanda.com – The Currency Site www.oanda.com/convert/fxhistory
[33] World Health Report 2001 - Annex Table 5 Selected National Accounts Indicators for all Member States. World Health Organization, 2001. http://www.who.int/whr/2001/en/whr01_annex_en.pdf
[34] *Questions Patients Might Ask About Kidney Transplant,* Mid-Atlantic Renal Coalition, 2002. [Mid-Atlantic Renal Coalition is one of 18 Medicare-funded organizations in the US responsible for improving the quality of care delivered to patients with End Stage Renal Disease.] http://www.esrdnet5.org/Transplant/ktqa/pts.pdf [Accessed 6/20/09].

They would not hold up to the scrutiny of business financials, let alone true economic analysis.

Two reasons seem to account for this. First, it may be because medicine has traditionally viewed economics and cost accounting with disdain. The medical establishment is now beginning to recognize the importance of the cost of care and is anxious to demonstrate this by publishing the relatively few studies that do cite monetary values. The second problem would appear to stem from the fact that while there are many prestigious clinicians for peer-review panels, there are few who also have the business and economic skills to appropriately evaluate the studies submitted for publication.

Surely, health insurers must have this data; after all, they have been paying for healthcare for years. Interestingly, Highmark Blue Cross Blue Shield, the eighth largest health insurer in the nation, did not set up a medical informatics department to analyze claims data until 1999.[35]

What is even more remarkable is that those other First World countries with nationalized healthcare systems are not much better. Why? Uncanny as it may seem, it is for the same reason that insurers in this country did not begin to collect that information— demographics! Enough healthy, young people working and paying in to the plans, so it was not really necessary to worry about costs. Other Western countries had the same post-war baby boom we did. When the demographics began to shift against all of us, the problems began to emerge.

---

[35] This was started by Donald E. Fetterolf MD, MBA, FACP (former Chief Medical Officer at Highmark); he is the current President of the American College of Medical Quality.

According to an Organization of Economic Development and Cooperation (OECD) report[36] these Ministries of Health (MOHs) in these countries are just beginning to mine national databases and compare health information.

> Many OECD member countries have already instituted national strategies to begin to collect quality indicators often for benchmarking purposes in a performance measurement setting. Those efforts have brought about much progress in implementing quality indicators for the level of providers, such as hospitals or physicians. *However, these national activities do not lead, except by accident, to internationally comparable QIs [Quality Indicators].* That is because there is a *lack of international agreement* on the *most promising indicators* and *many definitions of each indicator* that could be adopted. As published international health data sets such as OECD Health Data currently lack corresponding measures for national health systems, there is, so far, little possibility of international benchmarking of quality of health care. This deprives national policymakers of the opportunity to compare the performance of their health care delivery systems against a peer group.[37]

Choosing quality indicators presupposes an international standard of care for a given diagnosis. This is not surprising given the fact that *there is not even agreement on national standards in this country* for some of the most basic testing, let alone treatments for a condition. The US Guide to Preventive Services Task Force Guidelines show stark differences of opinion with the specialty groups regarding screening, diagnostic and treatment methods. When the numbers came

---

[36] Moise P. *Using hospital administrative databases for a disease-based approach to studying healthcare systems.* OECD Ageing Related Technical Report. August 2001 http://www.oecd.org/dataoecd/28/10/1889879.pdf
[37] OECD Healthcare Quality Indicators Project. Organization for Economic Cooperation and Development Web site [Accessed 8/4/09]. www.oecd.org/document/31/0,2340,en_2649_37407_2484127_1_1_1_37407,00.html

in, physicians following the specialty colleges' recommendations were overtesting, overtreating and unnecessarily worrying patients. The research did not back up the specialty standards. Proper standards of care become even more blurred when comparing recommendations of specialty groups across First World countries. It becomes apparent that there is no "gold standard"[38] of **clinically-effective, cost-effective care [ClE/CoE]** to use as a basis for judging the effectiveness of new or adjunct treatments.

It is vital to look at who is achieving the best clinical outcomes for the money spent to treat a given diagnosis, ClE/CoE care, along with the methods and processes used to deliver those outcomes. Only *after* that, can quality and quality indicators be determined. We have been putting the proverbial cart before the horse. ***Until we figure out who is getting patients better faster and cheaper, we don't have a standard for quality to use.***

About ten years ago while at the Director-General's reception during the World Health Assembly, I was talking with several ministers of health, who were lamenting the challenges of providing universal care. Among them was the French minister. He said, "America is the great healthcare experiment. Americans are a patient people. We, French, could never do to our people what you do to yours. If we did, there would be riots in the streets… We will let the Americans figure out what to do, and then we will just copy it." The others nodded.

---

[38] Typically, in medicine, the *gold standard* , as defined by Tabor's Medical Dictionary, is "medical care and experimental medicine, a therapeutic action, drug, or procedure that is the best available and with which other therapeutic actions, drugs or procedures are compared to determine their efficacy."

Aside from being a bit put off for a number of reasons, it was clear from that discussion that no other country was going to pick up the gauntlet and lead the charge. Other countries are financing their healthcare account deficits from other parts of their treasuries. Clearly, it is going to take old-fashioned American ingenuity to solve this problem.

What is needed is to take these catastrophic diseases and analyze the effectiveness of various First World nations' protocols for prevention, diagnosis and medical treatment as related to costs. Let us discover empirically who has found health. In doing so, the burden of disease both clinically and financially can be reduced.

This means engaging in multi-country, cross-comparative research on the most ClE/CoE treatments of the catastrophic diseases, since these have the greatest impact on the health care costs to the system. By working with Ministries of Health [MOHs] of other First World countries, comparing costs with health outcomes and treatments, we will discover who has a *competitive advantage* in treating a specific disease and why. In doing so, a truly **golden standard of care** may be established, founded in the best ClE/CoE medicine.[39]

In searching for health, no stone must be left unturned. The scientific method requires that scientific bias and national prejudice be set aside to reengineer medical treatment, including, but not limited to, evaluating emerging alternative and holistic therapies that show promise for improving patient care. Unfortunately, this most

---

[39] Here I propose a new term, the *golden standard of care* which encompasses an international standard of the most clinically-effective, cost-effective way to deliver healthcare.

basic scientific principle has not been readily applied to this aspect of medicine. Our goal is to definitively know what *is* the best medical care for the patients we serve. As better treatments and new discoveries are made, the *golden standard of care* will be continually redefined and re-established.

Chapter 4

Counting the costs

"How much is it?" does not seem to be a difficult question, but for some reason it is when it comes to healthcare.

The cost of an office visit

I cannot help but think the reason so many without insurance put off going to the doctor is the fear of how much it will cost. I believe this is the appeal of the "minute clinics" in pharmacies around the country. These clinics post a price list of services, usually by diagnosis. The prices are generally no more or less than what a physician will be reimbursed by an insurance company for an "established patient visit."[40] Yet for some peculiar reason, doctors still refuse to list prices. The argument is that we want to be

---

[40] "By CPT definition, a new patient is "one who has not received any professional services from the physician, or another physician of the same specialty who belongs to the same group practice, within the past three years." By contrast, an established patient has received professional services from the physician or another physician in the same group and the same specialty within the prior three years." Hill E. *Understanding When to Use the New Patient E/M Codes: Even an old patient can be new.* Family Practice Management, September 2003, p.33-36. http://www.aafp.org/fpm/20030900/33unde.pdf

professional and we do not like to talk about money.[41] Part of the resistance is also because we do not necessarily know the complexity of the office visit at the onset. Patients tend to put off going to the doctor and save up problems. As a physician, you may have thought you were going to examine a patient with a sinus infection, but by the time you leave the room you have treated their asthma, ulcer, hypertension and conjunctivitis. Obviously, this takes more time, energy and resources than treating a simple sinus infection. Patients can understand this. Rather than listing a diagnosis – doctors should list a level of office visit as we do for billing and give a few examples of diagnoses. That way, patients will have an idea what to expect. Often it is not the cost of the office visit, but *fear* of the cost and the *shame* in having to ask. The fear is "If you have to ask, you can't afford it" even if this is not the reality.

Why doctors cannot be charitable

This subsection is a bit of a digression, but it is important for patients to understand. Unfortunately, Medicare rules no longer allow physicians the luxury of compassion for patients down on their luck.

> Federal anti-kickback statutes prohibit providers from routinely waiving Medicare beneficiary fees, such as deductibles, coinsurance, or copayments. One rationale for the prohibition is "*the expressed intent of Congress that the <u>costs of services covered</u> by the Program will <u>not be borne by individuals not covered</u>, and the <u>costs of services not covered</u> by the Program will <u>not be borne by the Program</u>.*" The concern is that not collecting such fees or attempting to recover them might result in the costs being shifted to individuals not covered by Medicare…

---

[41] The rationale does not hold up when applied to other professionals. What architect designs a building and cannot give a cost estimate to build it? What engineer cannot give the cost to manufacture a machine he has designed?

The [Medicare] manual also says that routinely waiving the fees constitutes a reduction in providers' usual and customary charges, because their actual charges effectively become the full charges minus the patient fees. If providers are found to be engaging in such practices, Medicare may reduce their usual charges for all of their Medicare patients by the amount of the waived fees.

...the OIG [Office of the Inspector General] did not allow exceptions for...cost-based fee-for-service health care providers [doctors]...*the application of the statute to particular situations is often a matter of interpretation that requires a case-by-case analysis. This complexity can understandably leave providers confused about when the prohibition does and does not apply, and thus hesitant to ever waive fees.*

The clearest exception to the prohibition is one that allows providers to waive fees based on a particular patient's indigence. *It is the provider's responsibility to document indigence. According to Medicare guidelines, providers may consider as indigent Medicare beneficiaries who have been found eligible for Medicaid, or they may apply their customary methods for determining indigence as follows:*

1. The physician, not the patient, must determine indigence—a patient's signed declaration of inability to pay is not sufficient.
2. The provider should take into account a patient's total resources, liabilities, income, and expenses, as well as any extenuating circumstances.
3. The provider must determine that no source other than the patient is legally responsible for the patient's bill.
4. The provider must include in the patient's file documentation of how indigence was determined, as well as backup information to substantiate the determination.

According to the national office of the Centers for Medicare and Medicaid Services (CMS), a patient's indigence must be determined at *each* visit in which a coinsurance amount or deductible would apply, although it might be reasonable for a provider to use the same determination when the visits are within days of each other. According to the New England Medicare intermediary, indigence would need to be re-documented only when there is a change in the patient's status. In either case, ***these guidelines in effect require***

> ***providers to gather documentation in order to prove that they***
> ***should <u>not</u> be paid.*** [42]

What doctor has time to be a virtual credit reporting agency each time the patient walks in his office? To further slap kindness in the face, any physician found in violation of these regulations has committed a felony, punishable by a $25,000 fine and up to 5 years of imprisonment. This sort of offense is reportable to state licensing boards, malpractice carriers, health insurance carriers and hospitals; it will be essentially career ending.

Most doctors went into medicine to help people. They are willing to be compassionate when someone is needy. The law was intended to stop doctors from routinely waiving co-pays for the elderly, which many were doing as a courtesy, knowing these patients were on a limited income. In practice, the law affects *all* uninsured patients. As a Medicare contracted provider, providing a charitable discount to individuals not covered by Medicare is considered as effectively cost-shifting to Medicare. Instead of making it easier for people to get care, the unintended consequences of poorly thought-out laws have virtually prohibited doctors from being charitable. This is why the business of healthcare cannot be left to politicians.

The cost of a hospital stay

Prior to managed care which began emerging in California in the 1970s and spread to the rest of the country in the early 1980s, hospitals charged usual, customary and reasonable (UCR) fees for services. This was an itemized bill of goods and services used during a hospital stay. With

---

[42] Pryor C, Seifert R, Gurewich D, Oblak L, Rosman B, Prottas J. *Unintended Consequences: How Federal Regulations and Hospital Policies can leave Patients in Debt.* The Commonwealth Fund. June 2003.
http://www.passavanthospital.com/_data/files/pryor_unintendedconsequences_653.pdf

managed care came the concept of diagnostically related groups (DRGs). These were an attempt to control costs by allowing a hospital a given amount of money to cover the hospital stay for a given diagnosis. When DRGs were initiated, it helped cut down the number of days patients spent in the hospital, as hospitals sought to maximize profits. Patients no longer spend a week in the hospital for an appendectomy. Now, it's typically 23-hours.

Today, about eight different payment methods are used in an attempt to spread risk and keep costs down. Methods used vary by plan and carrier; often the same carrier may use different methods depending on the plan. Many plans use UCR charges minus a percentage discount. Discounts range from 20% to 60% for major plans, depending on market penetration; or they can be as little as 10% for smaller plans. The deepest discounts tend to be in areas where there is one large carrier which dominates the market. The deals negotiated between hospitals or preferred provider organizations (PPOs) and carriers or third party administrators (TPAs)[43] are a highly guarded secret. (See Chapter 11 – Those big, bad insurers.)

> Many corporate health plans have a record of the discount rate that has been negotiated with hospitals (e.g., 20%), but no record of the base prices that are to be used in the calculation of discounts. In fact, many TPAs claim that hospital prices are "confidential." When TPAs do not make that claim and attempt to acquire pricing from Preferred Provider Networks; they usually find that the Networks deem the prices "proprietary" and claim that corporate clients have no right to see the billing detail. In order to verify the accuracy of hospital bill charges, corporations must have a standard pricing schedule (e.g…"UCR"). Providers' discounts are applied to these prices.
>
> If a hospital wishes to treat Medicare and Medicaid patients, it is required to file its prices with the Federal Government. If pricing

---

[43] Third party administrators administer the health plans of companies large enough to self-insure for healthcare.

standards are <u>not </u>established, a hospital may inflate its prices by as much as 500%, before applying the negotiated discounts. In a publicly traded corporation, if no one knows what the prices <u>should</u> be; any certification of the adequacy of internal controls is misleading. In a worst case scenario, such certifications could be fraudulent.[44]

Companies must be careful they are not inadvertently handing their TPAs a blank check. While prices may be proprietary, there needs to be more transparency with the TPA's established clients, along with periodic independent auditing of the TPA.

To its credit, California began requiring hospitals to publish their UCR charges, also known as a "chargemaster" online. Table 1 below is from a Wall Street Journal article[45] that found the following price differences for some common tests and procedures:

Table 1

How Much Is That Chest X-Ray?

A new California law allows patients to look up the retail prices of many goods and services at hospitals. A survey of several hospital price lists shows dramatic differences in price.

	SCRIPPS MEMORIAL LA JOLLA, San Diego	SUTTER GENERAL, Sacramento	UC DAVIS, Sacramento	SAN FRANCISCO GENERAL, San Francisco	DOCTORS, Modesto	CEDARS-SINAI, Los Angeles	WEST HILLS HOSPITAL, West Hills
Chest X-ray (two views, basic)	$120.90	$790	$451.50	$120	$1,519	$412.90	$396.77
Complete blood count	$47	$234	$166	$50	$547.30	$165.80	$172.42
Comprehensive metabolic panel	$196.60	$743	$451**	$97	$1,732.95	$576	$387.18
CT-scan, head/brain (without contrast)	$881.90	$2,807	$2,868	$950	$6,599	$4,037.61	$2,474.95
Percocet* (or Oxycodone hydrochloride and acetaminophen) one tablet, 5-325 mg	$11.44	$26.79	$15	$6.68	$35.50	$6.50	$27.86
Tylenol* (or acetaminophen) one tablet, 325 mg	$7.06	No charge	$1	$5.50	No charge	12 cents	$3.28

*Hospitals carry either generic version, name brand, or both   **Represents the added total of 14 tests that make up the comprehensive metabolic panel
Sources: Scripps Memorial La Jolla; Sutter General; UC Davis Health System; San Francisco General; Doctors Medical Center; Cedars-Sinai Health System; West Hills Hospital and Medical Center

---

[44] Barber, J. *File NO. 4-511, Internal Control Roundtable (Sarbanes-Oxley Section 404)*. Security Exchange Commission Web site http://www.sec.gov/news/press/4-511/jwbarber2738.pdf [Accessed 6/20/09]

[45] Lagnado, L. *Medical Markup: California Hospitals Open Books, Showing Huge Price Differences*. Wall Street Journal; December 27, 2004, Page A1. http://online.wsj.com/article/SB110410465492809649.html [Reproduced with permission of the WSJ via Copyright Clearance Center.]

Making certain the correct chargemaster is applied for a patient given their plan is important and can make a considerable difference on the bill. Those most adversely affected by the lack of transparency in pricing have been the uninsured.

> As hospitals increasingly raised their charges and set prices by negotiating discounts from their chargemasters, those with the least bargaining power received the smallest discounts. An unfortunate consequence of this system is that self-payers, including the uninsured, were usually forced to accept the charges that hospitals stipulated. This created, probably inadvertently, a rather pernicious outcome in which patients who had the least ability to pay for their health care were charged the highest prices. This has resulted in considerable problems for some patients with very high health care personal debt, aggressive efforts at collection, and avoidance of needed services.

> In our interviews, hospital officials reported that they were reluctant to bill the uninsured for less than full charges because of insurers' common negotiating practice of insisting on being charged the same as the lowest-paying customers. They also cited Medicare guidelines and kickback regulations as reasons for not offering discounts to self-pay consumers. Related to this, they have operated with the understanding that they were subject to prosecution for fraud and abuse if they gave discounts without prior negotiation to any patients (even if they were poor and uninsured).

> Recently, adverse publicity has resulted in a clarification of Medicare rules that *does* permit hospitals to give larger discounts to low-income patients. Thus, many hospitals have recently adopted more systematic and proactive remedies to the financial problems faced by the uninsured and exacerbated by the inflated charges. These include granting the uninsured prices that are equivalent to common preferred provider organization (PPO) products or typical health maintenance organization (HMO) or other managed care contracts.[46]

---

[46] Tompkins CP, Altman SH, Eilat E. *The Precarious Pricing System for Hospital Services.* Health Affairs 25, no. 1 (2006): 45–56. http://content.healthaffairs.org/cgi/reprint/25/1/45

No doubt, there are still hospitals unaware of this clarification of policy,[47, 48] which is why it is included here. (The situation has still not been rectified for physicians.)

Unlike individual patients, insurers and TPAs generally know how much services should run. Outlandish overbilling will raise a red flag with a conscientious carrier or TPA. When negotiating a deal with a hospital or network, test scenarios will be run to see if the numbers look about right or not.

Frankly, debate over payment methods no longer really matters. At the end of the day, the hospital has to cover its expenses and show a little profit for reinvestment and return on investment (if a for-profit institution), or it will not be in business long. For the most part hospitals are doing this. All the various payment mechanisms have done is serve to confuse and distort the markets, making it more challenging to determine the actual costs for services. If the government, a carrier or TPA negotiates cheap rates for, say, imaging services (CT/MRI/pet scan), the hospital will make up for it by inflating other prices, leading to further price distortions.

Other revenue raising techniques

---

[47] Questions on Charges for the Uninsured. Centers for Medicare & Medicaid Services Web site http://www.cms.hhs.gov/AcuteInpatientPPS/downloads/FAQ_Uninsured.pdf [Accessed 6/20/09]

[48] Centers for Medicare & Medicaid Services Web site http://questions.cms.hhs.gov/cgi-bin/cmshhs.cfg/php/enduser/std_adp.php?p_faqid=7329&p_created=1148566371&p_sid=v6EoIxBj&p_accessibility=0&p_redirect=&p_lva=&p_sp=cF9zcmNoPTEmcF9zb3J0X2J5PSZwX2dyaWRzb3J0PSZwX3Jvd19jbnQ9MTUsMTUmcF9wcm9kcz0wJnBfY2F0cz0mcF9wdj0mcF9jdj0mcF9zZWFyY2hfdHlwZT1hbnN3ZXJzLnNlYXJjaF9ubCZwX3BhZ2U9MSZwX3NlYXJjaF90ZXh0PXVuaW5zdXJlZA**&p_li=&p_topview=1 [Accessed 6/20/09]

One of the major offenses a hospital can commit is "unbundling." It's punishable in a Medicare audit with exorbitant fines. Unbundling is billing for items separately when they should come as a package. For example, when a physician orders an analysis of serum electrolytes, a standard set of tests is performed simultaneously. In unbundling, that panel of tests is individually itemized in the bill. There is a line item for sodium, potassium, chloride, etc., as if each were ordered as a single test.

This also occurs with big ticket items, which come in a kit, such as joint replacement parts. Interestingly, although they come in a kit, you cannot go to the manufacturer's Web site to see exactly what that kit contains or how much any items cost. In fact, if you call the manufacturer or distributor, they will not give you the price of any items unless you are a board-certified orthopedic surgeon, and yes, they do look you up. Do you think there might be some collusion going on here? Where is the transparency? An honest hospital will supply a supplier's invoice with something close to the average wholesale price. We know facilities do not pay even average wholesale prices; discounts are awarded for bulk purchasing, prompt payment, etc. No one is against the hospital making a profit, but we would prefer it to be fair, as opposed to blind robbery.

It is interesting that with the rise in medical tourism, some American hospitals are now offering packages for a standard joint replacement that are much more competitive with their other First World counterparts abroad. It certainly pays to shop around for the facility, as well as to research the doctor who will be providing your care.

One feature regarding unbundling is never discussed and in fact may never even be noticed. This is in the area of charity care. Certainly not all hospitals are guilty of this, but a select few have employed this method of revenue protection, if not enhancement. Unbundling serves to inflate the amount of charity care those hospitals report, which is always good for public relations. If a for-profit hospital is doing this, it provides a bigger tax write-off. Quite clever, albeit unethical, isn't it?

Is more care better care?

More care is *not* necessarily better care.[49, 50] It does not necessarily result in better outcomes for the patient. Regional variations in frequency of office visits and lengths of hospital stay are independent of sickness levels. In fact, patients may be getting more care simply because there are more resources available to consult, or they may not have been getting the most appropriate care to adequately address their health problems in the first place.

Quality vs. cost — Does the best care cost more?

---

[49] Wennberg JE, Fisher ES, Goodman DC, Skinner JS. *Tracking the Care of Patients with Severe Chronic Illness: Dartmouth Atlas of Health Care 2008*. Dartmouth Institute for Health Policy & Clinical Practice.
http://www.dartmouthatlas.org/atlases/2008_Chronic_Care_Atlas.pdf
[50] Wennberg JE, Fisher ES, Baker L, Sharp SM, Bronner KK. *Evaluating the Efficiency of California Providers in Caring for Patients with Chronic Illnesses*. Health Affairs; Web Exclusive, November 16, 2005.
http://content.healthaffairs.org/cgi/reprint/hlthaff.w5.526v1?maxtoshow=&HITS=10&hits=1 0&RESULTFORMAT=&andorexactfulltext=and&searchid=1&FIRSTINDEX=0&resourcety pe=HWCIT

The short answer is "no." In fact, sometimes the best care costs less, because it is the best. Johns Hopkins Hospital is always on the top of the list of best hospitals in the country, yet it is often cheaper than many average hospitals.

By now you may be frustrated and think the whole process of trying to control costs is a sham, since the marketplace has been so distorted. On an individual basis, you might have an argument. We must approach the cost analysis of diseases based on the *average total claims paid data, rather than billed charges* for a given condition. *Claims paid are far more representative of the actual price tags, minus the distortions.*

Who is keeping tab?

A few years back, the Agency for Healthcare Research and Quality (AHRQ) started a database called Healthcare Cost and Utilization Project (HCUP). It is a database of inpatient *charges* and average length of stay by diagnoses or procedures. Unfortunately these are charges, not claims paid. The problem is that in doing so, AHRQ omitted the cost of physician charges, which average about 15% of any bill. It seemed odd that anyone would think such an omission insignificant. Thinking my staff and I must have misunderstood the explanation of the database, I sent one of my medical stop-loss nurses to Washington, DC, for a training seminar on it. In fact, AHRQ staff confirmed that physician charges were indeed excluded. Fifteen percent seems like a statistically significant number, but the rationale for their decision remains a mystery. While a given hospitalization has some interest, it is much less important than one might think, particularly at this stage of national healthcare planning.

Remember – It really doesn't matter what an appendectomy costs, only the catastrophic conditions count at this stage. This is where the big money is being spent. We need to make a big impact on costs fast, if we are going to maintain, let alone raise, quality. Once we tackle the big items, we can work our way backwards down to that appendectomy.

The real issue for underwriting purposes is, "What are the 1st and 2nd year costs of these catastrophic diseases and conditions?" This is important for how we will clinically manage patients, as well. Assessing costs begins not at the time a diagnosis is made, but from the time the person first had signs or symptoms of a problem, and the work-up, for what turned out to be the diagnosis began. *This is basic cost accounting. Unless this is done properly, with numbers and methods clearly spelled out, any further financial or supposed economic analysis is utterly and completely worthless.*

Interestingly, the first government agency to do this work was the Environmental Protection Agency (EPA) about 1999. It was trying to demonstrate the economic benefits to society of preventing one case of a given disease, such as bladder cancer. The information is published in the Cost of Illness Handbook. (See http://www.epa.gov/oppt/coi/) Where the EPA obtained its cost data is unknown, because even then, it seriously underestimated costs by at least a factor of two to three times, compared to actual claims seen. This is unfortunate, because the agency also underestimated the value of the work it was trying to demonstrate. It may have adversely affected policy development by undervaluing investments in prevention and safety by government and employers, leading them to pay more in healthcare costs.

In the private sector, the actuarial and consulting firm, **Milliman**, has a proprietary database of similar information. Table 2 (below) contains the cost information listed for transplants (in 2007 dollars):[51]

---

[51] Hauboldt, RH. *2007 US Organ and Tissue Transplant Cost Estimates*. Milliman. November 2007, Table 2. http://www.milliman.com/expertise/healthcare/publications/rr/pdfs/2007-US-Organ-Transplant-RR11-01-07.pdf

Table 2 - Estimated US Average 2007 First-Year Billed Charges per Transplant

Transplant	Procurement	Hospital	Hospital & Procurement	Physician	Evaluation	Follow-up	Maintenance Outpatient Immuno-suppressants	Total
	$	$	$	$	$	$	$	$
Heart	89,900	383,300	473,200	40,300	22,900	93,000	29,400	658,800
Single Lung	40,871	209,329	250,200	33,200	20,000	65,600	30,500	399,500
Double Lung	81,742	257,558	339,300	52,600	31,600	104,100	29,800	557,400
Heart-Lung	152,900	502,900	655,800	56,800	26,400	105,100	30,700	874,800
Liver	59,100	248,100	307,200	66,900	25,900	88,500	31,100	519,600
Kidney	58,300	74,500	132,800	21,500	14,600	48,000	29,500	246,400
Pancreas	66,200	107,100	173,300	24,600	14,700	48,300	36,400	297,300
Kidney-Pancreas	124,500	120,300	244,800	24,600	14,700	48,300	36,200	368,600
Bone Marrow – Autologous	21,249	134,951	156,200	21,700	19,800	75,400	-	273,100
Bone Marrow - Allogenic Related	24,223	253,177	277,400	13,700	20,500	145,200	21,800	478,600
Bone Marrow - Allogenic Unrelated	24,223	354,777	379,000	13,700	20,500	167,200	21,800	602,200
Intestine	75,449	602,451	677,900	87,100	41,700	78,500	23,400	908,600
Liver-Intestine	134,549	674,551	809,100	87,100	41,700	88,500	31,700	1,058,100
Liver-Pancreas-Intestine	200,749	587,751	788,500	87,100	41,700	88,500	35,100	1,040,900
Pancreas-Intestine	141,649	586,751	728,400	87,100	41,700	78,500	35,400	971,100
Kidney-Heart	148,200	419,200	567,400	40,300	22,900	93,000	35,100	758,700
Liver-Kidney	117,400	321,100	438,500	66,900	25,900	88,500	37,200	657,000
Other Multiorgan Transplants	143,493	516,307	659,800	66,900	31,600	105,100	36,400	899,800
Cornea	-	13,200	13,200	10,100	-	-	-	23,300

These are billed charges as opposed to claims paid. Generally insurers get a discounted package for the organ procurement and hospitalization, which lowers these costs by about 30% to 50%.

Compared with actual costs seen in claims data, in my experience, the other charges tend to be a bit inflated. But, it does give the upper limit of the normal range as a self-paying patient. Even with all the carrier discounts, you would have to agree that the costs are hideous at best, which is why we must determine the golden standard of care, as well the cost drivers.

A few years ago, **Medicare** proposed to collect treatment costs for various procedures from hospitals across the country, based on Medicare claims data for a specific DRG. It is important to remember that hospitals can still add charges outside of the DRG to the total bill. The database is called Hospital Compare.[52] Only a limited number of procedures are in the database, and consequently, it is of limited use.

Moreover, Medicare costs are not the best indicator because of unrelated comorbidities that tend to confound the cost data, as well as the frailty of the patients themselves. Because it tends to be cheaper for a person to die, than be kept alive, it is better to use the working age population. In addition, Medicare costs are heavily discounted versus the best of the private sector. According to the government database for the implantation of a pacemaker, Medicare *paid* approximately $13,700 dollars. However, Blue Cross Blue Shield of Tennessee states the following:

> …pacemakers range in cost from $35,000 to over $45,000. The additional cost of the procedure with associated medical care varies greatly depending on the place that the person receives the

[52] Hospital Compare. A Medicare Database: Department of Health and Human Services Web site
http://www.hospitalcompare.hhs.gov/Hospital/Search/Welcome.asp?version=default&browser=IE%7C8%7CWinXP&language=English&defaultstatus=0&pagelist=Home

> pacemaker. In an outpatient setting, where the procedure is done on the same day of discharge or the day prior to discharge, the average cost is over $2,000 plus the cost of the pacemaker...[53]

The latter is certainly much more representative of the claims data I have seen. This discrepancy raises a lot of questions for the government, hospitals and medical device manufacturers, particularly if this is truly what was paid.

Methods to achieve quality

There is much talk about effectiveness research in healthcare but it's generally about clinical effectiveness. The cost effectiveness research that has been done tends to be weak, because we do not necessarily know the most clinically effective treatments. For example, a cardiac patient will not necessarily live longer with a stent placed in his coronary artery than if he were medically managed with proper medications, diet and exercise. At this point, the two treatments are about equivalent.[54, 55, 56] As you can imagine, a

---

[53] *Medbrief: Pacemaker for the Treatment of Heart Failure.* Blue Cross Blue Shield of Tennessee Web site http://www.bcbst.com/learn/treatment-options/pacemaker.shtm [Accessed 6/28/09]

[54] Sculpher MJ, Smith DH, Clayton T, Henderson RA, Buxton MJ, Pocock SJ, Chamberlain DA. *Coronary angioplasty versus medical therapy for angina: Health service costs based on the second Randomized Intervention Treatment of Angina (RITA-2) trial.* European Heart Journal (2002) 23, 1291–1300. http://eurheartj.oxfordjournals.org/cgi/reprint/23/16/1291.pdf

[55] Džavík V, Buller CE, Lamas GA, Rankin JM, Mancini GBJ, Cantor WJ, Carere RJ, Ross JR, Atchison D, Forman S, Thomas B, Buszman P, Vozzi C, Glanz A, Cohen EA, Meciar G, Devlin G, Mascette A, Sopko G, Knatterud GL, Hochman JS. *Randomized Trial of Percutaneous Coronary Intervention for Subacute Infarct-Related Coronary Artery Occlusion to Achieve Long-Term Patency and Improve Ventricular Function.* Circulation. 2006;114: 2449-2457. http://circ.ahajournals.org/cgi/content/short/114/23/2449

[56] Hochman JS, Lamas GA, Buller CE, Dzavik V, Reynolds HR, Abramsky SJ, Forman S, Ruzyllo W, Maggioni AP, White H, Sadowski Z, Carvalho AC, Rankin JM, Jenkin JP, Steg PG, Mascette AM, Sopko G, Pfisterer ME, Leor J, Fridrich V, Mark DB, Knatterud GL. *Coronary Intervention for Persistent Occlusion after Myocardial Infarction.* New England

considerable amount of work must be done to determine what constitutes *quality care*.

On June 1, 2009, the American Medical Association, along with the American Hospital Association, the Advanced Medical Technology Association, America's Health Insurance Plans, the Pharmaceutical Research and Manufacturers of America, and the Service Employees International Union, sent a letter to President Obama proposing to lower healthcare costs by:

> Providing clinicians and other providers with the tools to address utilization and to improve quality and safety. [This] will help ensure that patients receive the right care at the right time in the right setting and will lower costs.
>
> [Developing]...performance measures to drive quality and promote better, more efficient care.
>
> [Sharing] best practices among hospitals, health systems and national, state, regional and metropolitan hospital associations.
>
> [Furthering] the use of known best practices, initially in the areas of infection prevention and patient safety and expanding over time into other areas.
>
> [Looking] at more effective approaches to health promotion and disease prevention, with a special focus on obesity.

These are lofty ideals, but there is no concrete way to reach them. Look carefully. None of these tools or performance measures have been developed yet. Only a few best practices are known, let alone universally disseminated and implemented. It will take decades to

Journal of Medicine. Vol. 355: No. 23; December 7, 2006.
http://content.nejm.org/cgi/reprint/NEJMoa066139v1.pdf

make a dent on healthcare costs if we have to develop performance measures and best practices from scratch. We need to know who has already found health and reverse engineer the process for our healthcare system.

Mechanics

To be of use, costs must be determined for the first and second years of a given catastrophic disease or condition. Most of those costs tend to occur early in the diagnosis. However, certain new biologic treatments, for example, entail significant ongoing maintenance costs.

As you will see in this book, all First World countries already are or will soon be facing the same demographic, medical inflation and medical claims problems we are. We should coordinate the process and methodology with other First World ministries of health (MOHs), as they also have an interest in finding health and lowering their healthcare expenditures.

We need other countries to do their own cost research for catastrophic diseases. All countries must agree to the methodology to ensure comparability. Unless a given comorbidity is unequivocally unrelated to the disease, it must be counted as part of the total costs of that disease for the year. Yes, some patients are sicker than others, but given enough cases we will begin to see two, or maybe three, clusters of costs. If we go back and look at the clinical data, generalizations can easily and quickly be drawn.

For a given condition or disease, we should then compare costs across the spectrum of nations. First, we must standardize for exchange rate differences, medical inflation (if comparing across years), and national health system discounts. The next step is to look at outcomes. This requires good clinical judgment. Life expectancy is an easy start, since these are "catastrophic" by nature. Are the outcomes similar or not? Is there a clear winner in clinical care? Outcomes should be limited and priority-weighted, so that the treatment goals are clear.

Globally, if we rank First World healthcare by cost and outcome, with clinical outcomes trumping costs, except where outcomes are equivocal, we would find who has already found health, hence the new *golden standard of care*. We need to organize a multinational group of experts, one per country, working on a given disease along with economists, pharmacists, chief nurses, underwriters, etc., to look at the cost and outcome information and determine who has found health.

In this country, we have an expert group that determines the standard of care in the rapidly changing field of oncology, the National Clinical Cancer Network (NCCN). It is an independent group of the leading researchers and clinicians in their respective areas within hematology/oncology. They write the treatment guidelines and best practices for cancer treatment. Approximately four times a year, they meet to review new studies completed and outline the clinical standards of care. Their work product includes a decision tree of appropriate treatment options given a patient's type and stage of cancer and treatment progress. The tree lays out equivalent options or therapies when there is more than one.

It may turn out that a country has an advantage is treating the very ill with multiple comorbidities, but not the standard patient. What is that country doing? Who is better at treating the standard patient and why? The panel needs to visit the best countries and determine what is included in the complete package of care, including nursing, home care and follow-up. This is an opportunity to share ideas and make care better even in the best countries, while reducing costs. The panel should determine who has found health for which patient segment. Those treatment protocols should become the golden standard of care. This group should write best practices and treatment guidelines from this information and distribute it via the Internet to national specialty colleges and their members, as well as to public and private insurers.

Panel members from the other First World countries need to see where they are deficient, and reverse engineer the process for their respective countries. Each expert should document and highlight for their colleagues what they specifically should be doing differently.

We do not have 40 years to figure out the determinants of quality by trial and error from the ground up. We need to know what already works and make it happen here. If we maintain an *unbiased* approach, it should become more evident what measures and indicators must be paid closer attention and what may be less important than we originally thought. Each new discovery or treatment would be judged by the *golden standard of care*. We should be able to prove cost-effectiveness and better outcomes as a result of our practice methods. Patients should benefit from better care for the dollars spent on them.

Each country should include the cost for various items to the treatment protocols developed so its providers start to grasp the cost of care. For example, if the costs of chemotherapy regimens and monitoring costs (i.e. PET/CT scan/Labs with periodicity) were listed for each treatment option, providers would be better able to contain costs themselves, all other things being equal. Providers must have some idea what costs are, if they are going to be of any help controlling them.

Why should we look at costs? We want the best quality -

Quality is a nebulous term, yet to be defined in healthcare. As the OECD has said, apparently it is challenging to get experts in a single country to agree let alone across countries. As we go through this exercise, we should begin to see what constitutes quality.

What we really want is the best value (outcomes) for our money. Costs give us a clear sorting variable. If we want the best bang for our buck, it is important to study them.

Costs can give some interesting insights into clinical management that might not be fully appreciated otherwise. [I would ask my clinical colleagues to keep an open mind and take a walk down the path with me.]

We can all agree that those patients who tend to run up high bills during their hospitalization were clinically very ill. But clinically, what are proven to be the most common drivers of costs for a given condition? They may also tell us what is driving the disease process.

When my medical stop-loss team[57] and I were working with the informatics department[58]at Highmark, we were initially trying to determine costs, and then if possible clinical predictors of costs from claims data. When we met with informatics again, they had taken various illnesses, and successively subdivided them by frequency of a patient's condition, status, age or comorbidity. These were given a "0" if we knew the patient did not have the given condition, status, age or comorbidity, a "1" if they did, and a "9" if we could not tell by the records. I have included a sample below for septicemia[59] (generally, not a catastrophic claim):

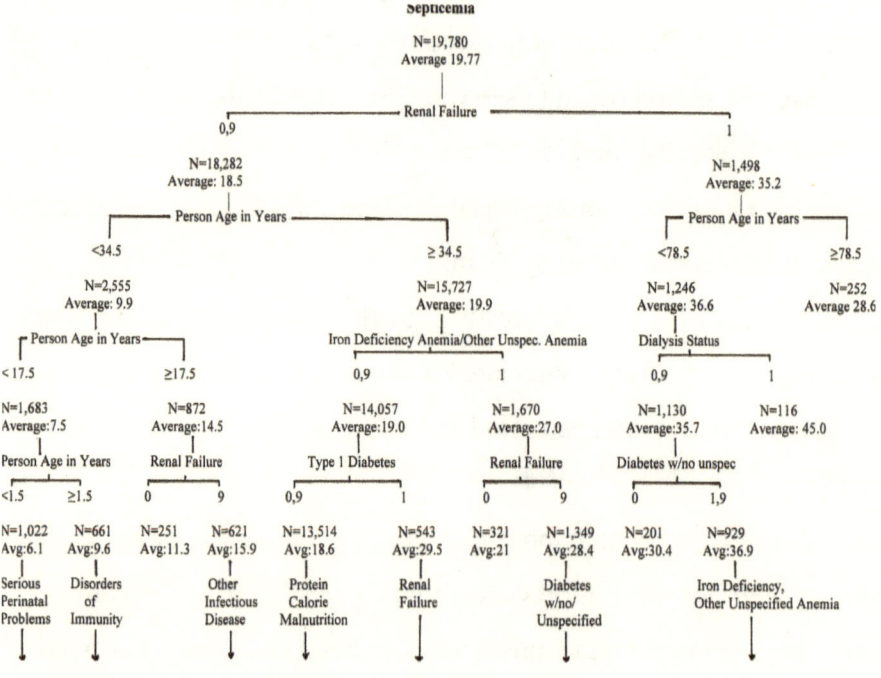

---

[57] Patricia Gladowski BSN, MSN, Tracy Mills RN, Patricia Suffern BSN, MPA and Lena Bretous MD, MPH
[58] Richard J. Pro MS, PAHM, Tom C. Schultz, Bryan Beatty and Christopher J. Scheib
[59] This information has no doubt changed in the last 6 years, with increasing drug resistances, as well as, the advent of new antibiotics and treatment protocols, but it demonstrates the logic.

N is the number in the sample. "Average" is a cost multiplier of a fixed amount X. In other words, overall patients with septicemia will cost 19.77 times (X). If they have renal failure, they will cost 35.32 times (X). If they are also less than 78.5 years of age, their costs will be 36.6 times (X). If they require dialysis, their costs will be 45 times (X). Now look at the other side of the nodal tree. If the patient either does not have renal failure or we cannot tell from the data, the next issue is if they are greater or less than 34.5 years of age. Take a look at the rest of the tree. Different conditions, ages and comorbidities become important drivers in different subgroups. This has important clinical management implications, as to how closely we may choose to monitor one group vs. another at certain points.

"Treat the disease, not the symptoms."[60]

Skyrocketing costs are mere symptoms of a sickly healthcare system. The focal point must be finding a better way of delivering healthcare and implementing it. We have thus far examined how to find health for an individual disease or condition. In the following chapters, we will examine how to find health for our healthcare system.

---

[60] This is a cornerstone tenet in osteopathic medical philosophy.

Chapter 5

Medical records, electronic & otherwise —The bane of our existence

Perhaps no other single issue has cost all of us - patients, providers, healthcare facilities and insurers - more time, frustration, money and misery than medical records or the lack of them. It has been said that waste, inefficiency and redundancy accounts for up to 30 percent of total spending and could be eliminated with no reduction in healthcare quality.[61] Reducing waste begins with secure but accessible medical information.

The extent of the problem

If you have gone to see a new doctor lately, the secretary making your appointment will tell you that you need to arrive a half hour early at your first appointment to fill out the necessary paperwork. Recently, a family member had an appointment with a specialist. The

---

[61] Delaune J, MD, Everett W. *Waste and Inefficiency in the U.S. Health Care System.* New England Healthcare Institute; February 28, 2008. http://www.nehi.net/publications/27/clinical_care_a_comprehensive_analysis_in_support_of_system_wide_improvements

office sent the papers ahead of time along with a letter stating that the patient should count on *45 minutes to an hour* to fill out the forms. Maddeningly, some of the same information was asked for multiple times on different pages. Hospitals are no better. Unless you arrive by ambulance, you will not see a doctor in the ER without going through the same sort of questions. While the information is necessary, surely there must be a way to streamline this process, without the waste of time and inconvenience.

How often have we seen a new doctor and forgotten, until the drive home, to mention some pertinent part of our medical history or a medication we had taken? We all have, at some point. Healthcare professionals are no exception. Many times patients go to an office or hospital for care and do not know, cannot remember, were not told, or did not fully appreciate their diagnosis or the medication given. They follow-up somewhere else, still ill and cannot tell the new doctor what was treated or how. That provider is left trying to guess what did not work.

The guesswork becomes particularly frustrating for the emergency room physician when an unknown patient arrives at the door with multiple illnesses and symptoms that can mimic much more serious problems. Since the doctor has no prior knowledge of what treatment or recent diagnostic testing the patient has received, he is forced to do the "million dollar workup,"[62] testing for and ruling out all the more serious problems, before he can treat the patient - in the end only to hear the patient say, "That's what the doctor at the other hospital told

---

[62] While not literally a million dollars, it is extensive and thereby also an expensive work-up, which must be done to rule in or out certain conditions given the symptomatology.

me."

I did my internship at Ohio Valley Medical Center in Wheeling, WV. Wheeling lies in the panhandle of the state along the banks of the Ohio River. Hospitals big and small are in each of the towns that line the Ohio, with two in Wheeling. In taking a careful history, usually when questioning the patient about any possible allergic issues with contrast media, the patient might let out that they had a given test at the other hospital in town. Upon calling the other hospital and having them fax copies of the patient's last visit, you might find that they had also been to a hospital further up river in Steubenville. Each hospital had done the same workup that was now being done, within days and sometimes hours of each other. It would turn out that the patient was really seeking a second or third opinion. While there is nothing wrong with getting another opinion, it could have been done much more simply, without the duplication of effort and waste of time, money and resources, had the ER physician had access to the patient's record of recent care.

Doctors often complain that insurers delay pre-certifying requests for diagnostic testing or procedures. Insurers today are generally not trying to deny every request, but they do have a responsibility to be good administrators of the plan, for the plan to remain solvent. What physicians may not appreciate is that their office staff may be unwittingly contributing to those delays. Their staff may not be aware of what the insurer needs, only forwarding the last office note without the pertinent patient workup evaluation or the notes containing the patient's history and symptomatology leading up to that workup. As a result, the nurse case manager (NCM) at the insurer is forced to attempt to chase the information down. The utilization review team, of which s/he is a part, may be forced by Utilization Review Accreditation Commission (URAC) standards to non-certify or withdraw the request if they do not receive the needed information in a certain number of days, as a result of noncompliance on the part of the office staff. A diligent NCM will often try to leave a message with the patient to have him attempt to reach his doctor's office to send in the requested information. This process might be understandable if it were a particularly unusual request, but that is often not the case. Too often, the request will come from, say, an oncologist's office for chemotherapy, without giving a stage of disease or specific drug or combination. Each stage has different treatments and often with multiple options. It would be financially irresponsible to the integrity of the health plan for the insurer to certify treatment without knowing what they are certifying. After all these years of managed care, it seems difficult to believe that this would still be a problem but it is a major issue. NCMs at insurance companies conservatively spend a third of their time trying to get the needed information. It all adds to the administrative costs of healthcare. The payors for healthcare services ought to have access to the records to provide the administrative services individuals and employer groups have contracted with them to provide under the plan.

Hospitals are often no better. Hospitals will often be vague about a patient's treatment protocol and "forget" to tell the insurer that this patient is in a clinical trial. Under such a trial, any costs for treatment

and monitoring that are outside the "standard of care"[63] treatment for
that disease are to be picked up by the study sponsor—usually a
pharmaceutical company, medical device manufacturer, etc. The NIH
lists all clinical trials in a searchable database on their website
www.clinicaltrials.gov. According to participation rules, hospitals are
not supposed to "double dip" —receive payment from the insurer and
the study sponsors, as it will compromise their ability to continue to
do studies. However, there does not seem to be a good way of
tracking compliance. Participants in clinical trials could be flagged if
there were a national medical record system. Perhaps more
importantly from a scientific standpoint, fewer patients who are
actively participating in clinical studies would be lost to follow-up by
the simple logistics of a household move. Their new doctors would
know what study and protocol was being used, who to contact and
what follow-up was needed.

Why the push for electronic medical records [EMRs] has failed -

At present, there is no universally accessible medical records
system in the United States. Despite having developed a national
office for Health Information Technology in 2006 and spending
billions of dollars, we are no further along in the process.

There is no good off-the-shelf Microsoft Office equivalent for
EMRs that could be exchanged relatively easily, let alone a secure
process to do it. The problem is that no one medical record system is

---

[63] In Oncology the NCCN Guidelines determine the standard of care for cancer treatment.

good for every level of healthcare. One company I worked for decided to try different medical record systems at each of their clinical sites to see which worked best. I happened to be covering several of their facilities at the time. If the first was cumbersome, each successive system seemed more onerous than the last. Keep in mind, this was just in clinics in the same medical specialty.

None of the systems on the market work well for all providers of care. Having reviewed many of the products of these systems while evaluating claims, I can tell you that most produce a poor quality record. The Veterans Administrator has been praised for having EMRs, but anyone who has ever seen a printout of those records would tell you they are far less than optimal. Apparently, most hospitals agree with me. Despite the fact that the VA's EMR system is open-source software, few have adopted it.[64] The National Health Service in the U.K. has an EMR system, which is only slightly better. (Its system was developed by GE Healthcare. Is it any wonder GE recently announced it will offer interest-free loans with deferred payments to help clinics purchase its products under the HITECH Act of the American Recovery and Reinvestment Act (ARRA)? [This is the federal stimulus spending bill.] The money is not available until 2011, "and the federal government has yet to set specific guidelines for determining what constitutes a 'qualified' system. To overcome these barriers to immediate adoption of EMRs, GE is…offering its

---

[64] Wagness, Lisa. *Few hospitals go paperless using free VA software.* Boston Globe, May 4, 2009.
http://www.boston.com/news/health/articles/2009/05/04/few_hospitals_go_paperless_using_f ree_va_software/

HITECH Warranty for Centricity EMR and Centricity Enterprise solutions and zero-interest funding with deferred payments to qualified buyers so they can have immediate access to this technology without the up-front capital costs.")[65]

Many hospitals have tried to develop their own medical records systems, some with more success than others. To its credit, Microsoft has a number of people working on the project. In fact, last year they purchased the EMR system developed by Bumrungrad Hospital[66] in Thailand.

The heart of the issue is that the different medical specialties and different facilities, such as hospitals, outpatient clinics and surgical centers, laboratories, have different needs. A small 28-bed rural hospital in Rosebud, South Dakota does not have the same needs as an academic medical center in a major metropolitan city. They provide very different services and levels of care. A urologist does not have the same needs in a medical records system as does an obstetrician or family practitioner. While all physicians may take a medical history, the focus may be very different. The standard diagnostic tests and procedures are also very different. Having a system that allows the physician to easily and correctly bill for these particular services is even more challenging.

These systems do not come cheaply. Besides the frustration of

[65] *GE launches program to accelerate EMR adoption.* GE Press Release, June 15, 2009. http://www.forbes.com/feeds/prnewswire/2009/06/15/prnewswire200906151308PR_NEWS_USPR____DC32606.html [Accessed 6/15/09]
[66] Bumrungrad Hospital is an internationally renowned hospital, accredited by the Joint Commission International, the international division of the Joint Commission of the Accreditation of Healthcare Organizations [JCAHO], which accredits US healthcare facilities.

trying to learn a new computer system, it may cost a physician's office $40,000 to $60,000 for a new system and $15,000 to $25,000 a year in maintenance fees. Avelere Health, a healthcare strategy consulting group, found the following:

> Using electronic health record (EHR) adoption costs published by the Agency for Healthcare Research and Quality (AHRQ), Avalere researchers found that a solo or small group physician practice will spend an estimated $124,000 over the five year period of 2011-2015 to adopt EHRs, and will receive up to $44,000 in federal incentive payments. The resulting financial deficit would be $70,000, or an average of $14,000 a year. This represents about 8% of this physician's annual Medicare receipts, contrasted with the legislation's provisions to impose an $8,500 penalty on non-adopters.[67]

It is not realistic to expect the solo practitioner to foot such a bill.[68] The bill for hospitals and healthcare systems can be a staggering line item expense. "Health information systems cost between $20 million to $100 million, depending on hospital size and complexity of the system. And many hospitals in the survey said they had no way of recouping that investment."[69] The President promises to give $19 billion to jumpstart the process, but as you can see the expenses are high and ongoing. Is it any wonder that only 13% of

---

[67] New Stimulus Incentives Raise Serious Health Information Technology Implementation Concerns 3/9/09 http://www.avalerehealth.net/wm/show.php?c=1&id=808 [Accessed 5/24/09]

[68] Conn J. *Rush for EHRs could 'stick docs with bad systems'* Modern Healthcare. Posted: April 30, 2009. http://www.modernhealthcare.com/apps/pbcs.dll/article?AID=/20090430/REG/304309994/-1&nocache=1&nocache=1 [Accessed 5/23/09]

[69] *Few US hospitals have electronic medical records.* By Julie Steenhuysen (Reuters). Wed Mar 25, 2009 5:00pm EDT http://www.reuters.com/article/bondsNews/idUSN2541283120090325 [Accessed 5/23/09]

offices[70] and 2% of hospitals[71] have comprehensive EMRs today?

While we have spent years trying to come up with "the ultimate, universal EMR," *this is* <u>*not*</u> *what we need or want for that matter.* Each type of provider and facility has different needs. It is not necessary for us all to use one system; we just need to have access to each other's records to care for the patient in front of us.

What will work

What we need is a national medical electronic filing cabinet to hold copies of our patient's records. In fact, we already have the means to put such a system together.

We need access to some basic information regarding the "unknown" patient before us, such as name, address, telephone, employer, emergency contact, insurance information, living will, etc. Upon verification of identity with a biometric identifier[72] in the provider's office or healthcare facility, the person becomes a "known" patient to the facility. Additional information regarding past medical

---

[70] *Electronic Medical Record Use by Office-Based Physicians and Their Practices: United States, 2006* by Esther S. Hing, M.P.H.; Catharine W. Burt, Ed.D.; and David A. Woodwell, Division of Health Care Statistics, CDC. http://www.cdc.gov/nchs/data/ad/ad393.pdf [Accessed 5/23/09] Note: Most use EMR for scheduling and billing, only about 13% actually use them for medical notes.

[71] *Few US hospitals have electronic medical records.* By Julie Steenhuysen (Reuters). Wed Mar 25, 2009 5:00pm EDT http://www.reuters.com/article/bondsNews/idUSN2541283120090325 [Accessed 5/23/09]

[72] Biometric identifiers, such as fingerprints or non-invasive iris imaging, have proven to be a rapid way to accurately identify a person; this technology is approved by the Transportation Security Administration (TSA) and is currently in use by Clear Card members in airports nationwide to speed through security lines. These devices should be small, portable and handheld peripheral particularly for use by paramedics, EMTs or ER personnel. If you are interested in reading more, please see this link http://www.cbc.ca/news/background/airportsecurity/biometrics.html .

and surgical history, current medications, allergies and side effects to medicines, and family and social history would then present itself to the provider. This information could be verified and updated by the provider on each office visit. Some organizations have proposed *patient*-input systems. In fact, the AMA has sponsored one. However, as anyone who has ever read a patient-reported history will tell you, it is often incomplete with misspellings and inaccuracies that may be detrimental to care.

We would need to verify that those offices and facilities accessing the system were indeed legitimate providers. It should be able to tell that the computers used were from those offices, and it should be able to identify which staff member accessed the system. In essence, providers would be credentialed. It seems that we do similar types of verification with systems like PayPal, which acts as an electronic facilitator for e-commerce. It is a private company with the technological means to assure and maintain the security of financial transactions. It seems that we need a similarly credible organization to *bank* healthcare "transactions" or visits. It would seem desirable for there to be more than one such organization for security. However, more than a half dozen may needlessly slow down accessing the complete patient record. A decentralized national filing cabinet should have a standardized overarching format for such "transactions." Much like Visa which has many banks, it is the Visa product platform through which services are delivered. When biometrically identified, the EMR platform would use that information to validate and tap into *all* of the authorized EMR banks, assembling the complete EMR for the patient and delivering it to the provider's screen, similar to the way credit bureaus use your social security number to assemble a credit report. No matter which "bank" a given provider chooses for its transactions, the feel for the end user would be the same. Accounts for "known" patients to the provider or facility, would automatically receive reports sent from other providers and consultants, laboratories, etc. The full EMR should be viewable to the provider for several hours after being biometrically identified, so that the provider could have access to read up on his patient at the end of the day. Similarly, if the patient is in the ER, the record would be available for a number of hours before the patient is admitted. Obviously on admission, the full EMR should be available until discharge.

The full EMR would list a tab for recent provider visits with the dates of service, provider, specialty and billed diagnosis with a link to a read-only copy of the medical record for that visit. Other tabs for laboratory tests and diagnostics would show dates of service, providers, tests ordered and diagnoses with a read-only access link to the results is also needed. The diagnostics tab should also include the electronic imaging for areas such as radiology, pathology. Each provider or facility would be responsible for inputting its information into the system for that patient visit by the end of the day. The full record is "open" because the patient was there and properly identified; otherwise, the facility would only be able to access a "known" patient's basic record and reports specifically routed to them. Offices and facilities with EMRs should input a read-only copy of the visit that would automatically dump into the full EMR for that patient. Those facilities still using paper could PDF their documents into the system. Initially, handwritten documents may be allowed. Ideally, the goal would be for notes to be typed to eliminate the hieroglyphics. This would also allow universities, with proper permissions secured and individual identities masked, to do aggregate research on certain diagnoses. Optical recognition software (ORS) could be used to scan documents, for say, symptoms, treatments or findings, rather than painstakingly sorting through each page by hand as is done now.

As hard as we try, when human beings are involved, errors may occur in the input process. Pages may not be scanned properly. Edges may get cut off. If a person has a common name, it is not impossible for the practice or facility to have two people in the practice with the same name seen on the same day. (It has happened to me.) Records can be put in the wrong EMR if it is still "open." It would seem that if there is a suspected problem with an EMR, there should be a check box at the end of each line containing that office, hospital, lab or diagnostic visit to indicate that. When another credentialed entity spots a problem and ticks the box, a pop up with the question, "What is the problem?" allows the user to identify it. A message would be triggered for the entity that had originally input that information that there is a situation needing to be addressed. The entity would be given perhaps a week to fix the problem, or one of the "banks" may charge it, say, $50 per day, until the problem is addressed.

Perhaps one day we will have a favorite EMR for the urologist, another for the obstetrician and yet another for the family practitioner. Perhaps there will be an EMR for each hospital type and size. But I believe we are a good half dozen years away.

Meanwhile, it seems that a system similar to what I have proposed here would only require a high-grade optical scanner (certain minimum requirements with ORS capabilities), a biometric scanner, along with an office computer and internet service provider. Most offices already have computers and ISP service, for less than $600 extra, an optical scanner and biometric scanner may be purchased. Access to the patient's EMR would cost perhaps a penny or two to the user. This is much more realistic for a solo practitioner, and is certainly a much less burdensome expense for the even the major academic medical center.

Most importantly, it also gets the job done for the patient! It allows the patient to get the care needed in a timely manner, while eliminating redundancy and waste in the system.

Chapter 6

Becoming better doctors

The costs of providing state-of-the-art medical care are increasing. Patients believe it is their right to receive the best healthcare available regardless of cost. Physicians believe they should be able to provide the best care possible, regardless of the bean counters at the insurance companies and in government. Oddly, it seems this frustration is common in the industrialized world, whether there is a state insurance system or private insurance; physicians feel the care they are able to offer could and should be of better quality.[73]

Physicians often feel that they are at wits end trying to run a medical practice today, between increasing regulatory demands, ever-changing reimbursement rates for a given code or service, and increased professional expectations often placed upon them by malpractice carriers, state medical boards and specialty medical boards.

---

[73] Blendon RJ, Schoen C, Donelan K, et al. *Physicians' view on quality of care: a five country comparison.* Health Affairs 2001; 20(3): 233-243.

As if that were not enough, every year for the past several years, physicians have been threatened with a decrease in their pay under Medicare's Sustainable Growth Rate Formula for reimbursement for services provided.

> If the SGR formula is not fixed, physicians will receive negative updates of approximately five percent each year from 2006 until 2013 and rates will not return to their 2002 level until well after 2013. [See graph below.] In other words, physicians will receive less reimbursement in 2013 than they did in 2002 for the exact same procedure, regardless of inflation and increases in practice costs. Indeed, while reimbursement will likely be cut by over 30 percent under the current formula, it is estimated that costs for providing services, as determined by the Medicare Economic Index (MEI), will rise by close to 20 percent. Such cuts will further inhibit each physician's ability to provide services to Medicare beneficiaries as many physicians will simply be unable to afford to treat Medicare patients. [74]

Medicare Physician Payment vs. Medicare Economic Index (cost of providing services)

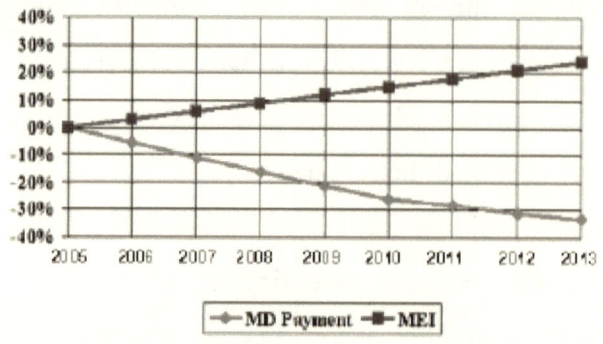

Adapted from the American Academy of Orthopedic Surgeons Website [75]

---

[74] Issue Brief: Medicare Physician Payment Fixing the Sustainable Growth Rate (SGR) Formula. Alliance of Specialty Medicine. American Academy of Orthopedic Surgeons Web site http://www.aaos.org/Govern/public/Medicare/SGRissuepaper_Hillbriefing.asp [Accessed 5/23/09]

[75] Ibid.

Each year the American Medical Association and American Osteopathic Association have to lobby Congress to "fix" the formula for that year, which requires passing a law for an "adjustment" which gets it back to where it was the year before, with perhaps a 1% to 2% increase. As you can see from the graph above, this is still a pay cut, as it is not enough to even match a cost of living adjustment for the practice. In addition, a 21% pay cut is scheduled for January 1, 2010, if Congress does not pass a "fix" this year.[76] Few businesses could be expected to sustain that kind of hit to their bottom line. Physicians are quickly becoming the ultimate "market takers." [77]

Compounding the problem, a physician shortage is projected for the United States over the next 10 years.[78] The woes of the malpractice crisis are causing physicians to move from high risk states to lower risk ones; to limit their practice to lower risk patients requiring lower risk procedures; or simply to retire from practice. The financial uncertainty of an ever-evolving health insurance reimbursement process has led Inc. Magazine[79] to call medicine "the worst business in the country."

Most doctors just want to practice medicine and not be burdened with all of these business issues. They bring on additional staff hoping

[76] Cys J. *Running out of patches? Options for fixing the Medicare pay crisis*. American Medical News; January 5, 2009. http://www.ama-assn.org/amednews/2008/12/29/gvsa1229.htm

[77] Market takers are not influential enough to set prices, unlike market makers.

[78] Croasdale M. *Federal advisory group predicts physician shortage looming; Council on Graduate Medical Education reverses stance, calls for 15% increase in medical school graduates*. American Medical News; November 3, 2003. http://ama-assn.org/amednews/2003/11/03/prsbl1103.htm

[79] Weyrich N. *The worst business in America*. Inc. Magazine 2003;12: 80 or for online version http://pf.inc.com/magazine/20031201/theworst.html [Accessed 5/23/09]

that will solve the problem and allow them "more time to do their job" —taking care of patients. Usually this does not work as well as they would like it to.

Having watched my colleagues go through this process, it has become apparent that our physicians are ill-prepared to set up and run their own practices. When most physicians finish medical school and three or more years of postgraduate training in internship and residency, they have no idea how to set up an office. Most join established practices, with lower pay, simply to try to figure out, as best they can, the business of medicine. After a few years, they may try to strike out on their own. Unlike chiropractors, physicians receive little or no training in medical school on how to set up and run an office. It does seem unbelievable that despite having saddled the average medical student with more than $142,000 in debt[80], medical schools have yet to realize they have an obligation to teach their students about the business of starting and running their own medical practices. What's more, specialty colleges offer little or no training, perhaps it is because they are run by physicians who themselves have had little formal training. The other reason may be because it is difficult to get approval for continuing medical education for anything that is "nonclinical." The naive notion that learning how to more efficiently utilize your human and material resources, to run a more

---

[80] "All told, 17.7 percent of graduates had educational loans of $200,000 or more—more than triple the 4.9 percent who had that amount in 2004. Students with debt levels between $175,000 and $199,000 rose a full percentage point from 2007 to 2008, with nearly nine percent of 2008 graduates in this category. Students reported an average debt load of $141,751, more than $10,000 higher than 2007 GQ data." AAMC Reporter: December 2008: Graduates Report Higher Debt, Primary Care Interest http://www.aamc.org/newsroom/reporter/dec08/graduates.htm [Accessed 5/23/09]

cost-efficient medical practice, is not viewed as clinically relevant.

Is it any wonder physicians are notoriously known as poor businessmen? Have you tried to make an appointment or called your doctors office? Most of the time, you can consider yourself fortunate to speak with another human being. How many times have you been to an office or healthcare facility where the staff hides behind a glass window ignoring you standing there for several minutes? There is usually a sign taped to the window that says, "Please do not knock on window." It is both frustrating and de-humanizing. I have family who worked for the airlines back in the day when flights were still a luxury. TWA told its employees: "Treat our customers well. The only thing we have to offer is service." If only we ran our offices and hospitals with that same logic.

The myth that all providers are created equal

This idea seems to be propagated more strongly than ever by non-physician groups who are seeking an expansion of practice rights. While physicians are facing ever increasing expectations regarding hours of continuing medical education and board re-certification exams every 7 to 10 years, there is a push by politicians and non-physicians groups to address the healthcare shortage by having far less qualified professionals doing a physician's job. How can a physician's assistant (PA), who has had two years of general college and two years of clinical training be equal to a physician with four years of college, four years of medical school and three or more years of residency? The PA program began out of the military medic program. They are to be the physician's assistant. *They are not and should not be viewed as a replacement for a physician.* They do not have the depth of training. They have a very important place in healthcare, but not how they are traditionally used.

In fact, only one physician I have ever worked with, either in my training or in practice, really knew how to utilize these professionals—that is James Laws, DO, an interventional cardiologist from Dayton Ohio. He is a very fine physician and human being, about whom the 2006 documentary movie "Beyond the Call"[81] was made. I had the good fortune to train with Dr. Laws while in my fourth year of medical school. Dr. Laws had an incredibly busy clinical practice. He typically had at least 40 patients in Grandview Hospital at any given time, along with a few patients in the smaller Southview Hospital. He would send at least two of his PAs ahead of him to the hospital to gather and organize all the labs, diagnostic testing and consult reports and make preliminary rounds on his patients to see how they were doing. Before he left the office, he would call his PAs and say, "I'm coming." He was notorious for charging through the hospital wards, with his PAs running with charts in hand to catch up. But, when he walked into a patient's room, all his attention was on that patient.

Patients would wait patiently for him all day long because they knew when he got there, they were *the* center of his attention. He spent his *entire* time looking at and talking to the patient. As he examined them, he gave the PA his findings. His PA read off the

---

[81] *Beyond the Call*, Movie Web site http://www.beyondthecallthemovie.com/ [Accessed 5/22/09]

results of the labs, diagnostics and consults. He gave them that day's orders and answered the patient's questions. Before he left the room, he reviewed the PA's note. Because Dr. Laws' staff knew his standard operating procedures and practice, they had the clinical results ready for him. He could focus on his patients when he was with them, maximizing his time with them. Another PA would meet him in the hall and brief him on the next patient he was going to see.

Years later, I was doing contract jobs in southwestern Ohio. When I would work in a new location, people would ask if I had ever lived in the area, and I would tell them I had trained with James Laws DO, in Dayton. Invariably, everyone knew of Dr. Laws and raved about him. In fact, you would hear things like their mother-in-law's brother's wife had Dr. Laws as her cardiologist, and what a wonderful doctor he is and what great humanitarian work he does as well. I have never known any other doctor who has such a sphere of influence, with as many degrees of separation as he does. No doubt, it is because he does not waste time getting caught up in the madness of the paper chase in medicine today; he leaves that to his PAs. His PAs make certain all the necessary pre-certifications are in place. Patients believe they are cared about, *and they are*. Dr. Laws listens to his patients and does what he was trained to do, be the best interventional cardiologist in southwestern Ohio.

Unfortunately, that is rare today. Our doctors are bogged down in documentation and paperwork unnecessarily. This is what the PAs and nurse practitioners (NPs) should be doing. Doctors should be seeing the patients and supervising the documentation of those visits, not buried under it.

Physicians need to be better managers of themselves and their staff, instead of the secretary at the front desk who is often managing the doctor. Physicians need formal management training in medical school. They also need to understand how to work within the healthcare system. One of the greatest difficulties hospital executives have today is disruptive physician behavior. We cannot have doctors who think they are so brilliant that patients and co-workers should have to put up with their perennial bad behavior. The smart but obnoxious Dr. House model (from the Fox television show) should be shunned. Being a great diagnostician and technically proficient doctor is more than important; it is *vital* for professional credibility—make no mistake about it. But, it is only the first, lowest step in professional development, rather than the capstone. We need physicians who are capable of becoming more. Medical schools may need to perform psychological testing on applicants to ensure that they are well-balanced human beings before accepting them. Do you want people with dependencies to have access to prescription drugs? Or doctors with personality disorders making moral and ethical decisions regarding patient treatment? All health professionals should undergo testing as part of the admission process. A young Dr. House will never get in, a young Dr. Laws will.

Problem doctors

Despite over a quarter of a century of managed care in this country, we still have physicians who are determined not to work with the insurer for their patient's care. They believe their order for a test should be good enough. Too many still do not do the proper workup on their patients before requesting pre-certification for a procedure.

There are a small but significant number of physicians today who seem to be looking for a body to do a procedure on. I believe this may be due to their lack of moral compass, because there is often absolutely no medical need for the procedure as verified by outside same-specialty peer-review. One example was a request for an insured gentleman to have a penile implant. He had tried various impotence drugs over the past year without success. His past medical history included hypertension and diabetes. He had seen his primary care physician (PCP) and a urologist, the latter of whom was making the request. We asked the insured if there had been any change in his antihypertensive medications over the last year, to which he answered no. He had been on the same medications for a number of years. We noticed there was no blood pressure taken on his PCP visit notes. A day or so later, when we received his urologist's notes, again there was no blood pressure reading. Given that hypertension can contribute to impotence, one would hope that a healthcare professional might check it before recommending such a radical procedure, particularly since they each noted he had hypertension in their notes.

It can only be attributed to a lack of moral compass that transplant teams at major medical centers approve alcoholic patients *still in treatment* for liver transplants ($393,000 for first year treatment costs according to actual claims paid data) when previously we required them to demonstrate six months of sobriety.

Ethical standards need to be applied and enforced by medical boards. In 1999, the American College of Obstetricians and Gynecologists issued ethics guidelines regarding treatment for infertility that urged doctors to limit the number of embryos transferred as part of in-vitro fertilization and to cease fertility drug treatment after one egg is released. Nevertheless, we still have practitioners who are determined to get a baby out of the process, no matter the cost to the mother, children or society. While fertility treatments may not be covered by a health plan, the costs of these multiple births *are* covered, since they are now members of the mom's health plan. We know that "most couples (about 84 out of every 100) who have regular sexual intercourse (that is, every 2 to 3 days) and who do not use contraception will get pregnant within a year. About 92 out of 100 couples who are trying to get pregnant do so within 2 years. For women aged 35, about 94 out of every 100 who have regular unprotected sexual intercourse will get pregnant after 3 years of trying. For women aged 38, however, only 77 out of every 100 will do so. The effect of age upon men's fertility is less clear. If you have not been able to get pregnant after 2 years of regular unprotected sexual intercourse either one, or both, of you may have a fertility problem."[82] We need to question why the medical definitions for infertility in this country has shifted from two years attempting to have a baby to one. We also need to question why artificial

---

[82] *Understanding NICE guidance – information for people with fertility problems, their partners and the public.* National Institute for Clinical Excellence, February 2004. http://www.nice.org.uk/nicemedia/pdf/CG011publicinfoenglish.pdf

reproductive treatments are being used for young women who may just need time.

A small number of providers either do not seem to know when to refer a patient or choose not to do so. A disability case I reviewed comes to mind. The gentleman had a well-paid, highly responsible executive position with a large company. Unfortunately, he had a terrible trigeminal neuralgia. He was treating with a neurosurgeon for about a year at the time, without success. Since we had no recent notes, I had the NCM call the physician's office to get the treatment plan and see if he was going to do a certain procedure which would have had a success rate of over 90%. She said the nurse asked the doctor, who told her that he does not do that procedure. He was going to continue the same treatment, which included medication that left the patient so snowed that he had been unable to work for the past year. This surgeon had no intention of referring this poor gentleman to someone who could help him get back to living his life. I guarantee this gentleman did not want to be disabled.

Doctors need to understand the value of the tests they order

The most recent trend is for physicians to order a coronary CT angiography (CTA) with calcium score for their asymptomatic patients to screen for coronary artery disease (CAD). The score is supposed to quantify the amount of atherosclerosis present in the arteries. The problem with this test is that we do not know what these arbitrary "scores" actually mean. "An assessment of the literature on calcium scoring by the German Agency for Health Technology

Assessment (DAHTA, 2006) concluded that measuring coronary calcium is a 'promising' tool for risk stratification, but that many questions remain unanswered about the targeted use in medical practice, including which patient groups should be screened, which calcium score threshold should be applied, and which scoring method should be used."[83]

An assessment by the Ontario Ministry of Long-Term Care Medical Advisory Secretariat (MAS, 2007) found insufficient evidence for the use of coronary CTA as a screening test for CAD in asymptomatic individuals. The assessment found that coronary CTA exhibits only moderately high sensitivity and specificity for detection of CAD in an asymptomatic population. If population-based screening were implemented, a high rate of false positives would result in increased downstream costs and interventions. Additionally, some cases of CAD would be missed, as they may not be developed, or not yet have progressed to detectable levels. The assessment noted that there is no evidence for the impact of screening on patient management.

...A decision memorandum from the Centers for Medicare & Medicaid Services (CMS, 2008) has concluded that there is uncertainty regarding any potential health benefits or patient management alterations from including coronary CTA in the diagnostic workup of patients who may have CAD. The memorandum stated that no adequately powered study has established that improved health outcomes can be causally attributed to coronary CTA for any well-defined clinical indication, and the body of evidence is of overall limited quality and limited applicability to Medicare patients with typical comorbidities in community practice. The memorandum noted that the primary safety concerns with cardiac CTA are the exposure to radiation and the use of contrast and ß blocker medications.

---

[83] Aetna Corporate Policy Bulletin
http://www.aetna.com/cpb/medical/data/200_299/0228.html [Accessed 5/23/09] Reprinted with permission of Aetna Inc.

The CMS decision memorandum (CMS, 2008) explained that cardiac CT angiography is unlikely to benefit persons at high risk for CAD, as these persons will likely need to have invasive coronary angiography regardless of the results of this test. The CMS decision memorandum also stated that there is no evidence that CT angiography will benefit persons with chest pain at low risk of CAD…The decision memorandum observed that, in systematic reviews of coronary CT angiography, the overall reported sensitivity, specificity and predictive values are generally above 80 to 90 percent (CMS, 2008). The decision memorandum stated, however, that these estimates have limitations in applicability and generalizability due to patient selection and potential bias. The decision memorandum found no published studies of the sensitivity and specificity of coronary CT angiography in persons at low or intermediate pretest probability of CAD. Although available studies have not consistently reported the participants' pretest probability of CAD, almost all persons enrolled in these studies are likely to be at relatively high risk for CAD, since they were already scheduled for invasive coronary angiography. The decision memorandum noted that, in general, test sensitivity and specificity will be higher in patients with more severe disease…The CMS decision memorandum also explained that the reported positive and negative predictive values of coronary CT angiography based on high risk patients are not directly applicable to low or intermediate risk patients because the prevalence of disease is different (CMS, 2008). The predictive values would very likely be lower if calculated using data from low or intermediate risk patients since these populations have a lower prevalence of CAD.[84]

If there is no impact on patient management as a result of the screening tests, there is no point in doing it. As you can see the Germans, Canadians and our own Centers for Medicare & Medicaid Services (CMS) all came to the same conclusion. Yet practitioners continue to make such requests on behalf of their patients. Doctors need to know the costs of the tests they order and understand when the evidence base supports ordering a given test for a given patient.

[84] Ibid.

Physicians must understand the power of one test vs. another to get the biggest bang for our healthcare dollars. Otherwise our good intentions will cost the system more money and our patients more worry, both unnecessarily.

Physicians need to have a better understanding of epidemiology and biostatistics to better evaluate the quality and results of the studies they read and to know what questions they should be asking presenters in continuing medical education seminars.

Public health and the business of medicine

We must change the way our physicians are trained so that they are capable of meeting the demands of today's healthcare system. We need physicians with a solid understanding of public health and the business of good medicine. These principles need to be integrated into medical education. There must be educational reform. There are ways to do so without adding extra years to the educational process. This subject requires more space than can be allowed in this book, but I would be remiss not to mention it. Physicians must be able to think systemically and still treat the patient in front of them. They must be more than great technicians. We need physicians with the tools to lead the needed process improvements in medicine. We need to train leaders who encourage their fellow healthcare professionals and are looking for ways to work together to find better answers to the issues we face now and in the future.

Chapter 7

Becoming better patients

Many well meaning people have not seen a doctor in years, primarily because they do not want to be a hypochondriac like …. Fill in the blank with the name of whatever family member who nearly drove the rest of the family to madness complaining of their real or mostly imagined symptoms and illnesses.

Patients have the greatest responsibility for their own health. No one else has more to lose. This is _not_ being a hypochondriac. Good health is so often taken for granted, until it is not there.

As an occupational medicine physician, I have done many pre-employment physicals. These exams are generally on healthy people who have been offered a job contingent on passing the physical. Most of the time, they are fairly healthy. But on occasion, I will find new-onset diabetes, hypertension, skin cancer, poor lung function (usually due to a history of smoking for more than 10 years) or any number of other problems. I tend to find most of the patients with positive findings do not have a personal physician or have not seen a doctor in years. When asked why, they generally say "I am healthy," or "I don't want to be a hypochondriac like…" More goofy family members have stopped patients from getting preventive check-ups and early diagnosis than any lack of health insurance.

Patients have an obligation to themselves to have a *periodic preventive health examination* as recommended by the US Guide to Preventive Services Task Force (USPSTF).[85]

> The … [USPSTF] is an independent, non-governmental panel of experts in prevention and primary care that is convened by the Agency for Healthcare Research and Quality (AHRQ)…[It] conducts rigorous, impartial assessments of the scientific evidence for the effectiveness of a broad range of clinical preventive services, including screening, counseling, and preventive medications… [evaluating] the benefits and harms…in healthy populations based on age, gender, and risk factors for disease and …[making] recommendations about which preventive services should be incorporated routinely into primary care practice. In making its recommendations, the USPSTF assesses the quality of evidence supporting a specific preventive service and the magnitude of net benefit in providing the service. [86]

You can find those recommendations by plugging in your basic health information into its Web site.[87] There is also information on what those tests entail if you click on the "Tools" section. These tests have been shown to be of value in finding and maintaining health. Your physician may have reason to order additional tests based on your history and physical examination, but you need to make certain

---

[85] Electronic Preventive Services Selector, Agency for Healthcare Policy & Research Web site http://epss.ahrq.gov/ePSS/introduction.jsp [Accessed 6/21/09]
[86] Electronic Preventive Services Selector, Agency for Healthcare Policy & Research Web site http://epss.ahrq.gov/ePSS/about.jsp [Accessed 6/21/09]
[87] Electronic Preventive Services Selector, Agency for Healthcare Policy & Research Web site http://epss.ahrq.gov/ePSS/GetResults.do?new=true [Accessed 6/21/09]

you get the healthcare you need. This is not being a hypochondriac; it is taking charge and being responsible.

Going to the doctor

It is odd that we spend probably a year or so in grammar school studying health, including the food pyramid and learning where our spleen is, but no one ever teaches us how to be good patients. This is the most important thing we could learn in such a class!

Having worked in the former Soviet Union, in Russia, Georgia and South Ossetia, I cannot say much good about their healthcare system. The book, <u>Cancer Ward</u>, by Alexander Solzhenitsyn describes a typical Soviet facility quite accurately. However, the one thing the Soviets did manage to do exceptionally well was to teach patients how to give their doctors a good medical history, in a logical and orderly way. Even working through an interpreter, it was easier to take a medical history there than it is here.

Most people can tell you they are sick, but it takes forever to get them to tell you when it began (sometimes who else in the family or at work got it first), what they tried, what worked, what didn't, etc. They generally only answer the questions asked and do not tend to volunteer any information they think might be important because the doctor didn't specifically ask for it. Then there are invariably the small but significant number of patients who when asked, "What brings you in today?" say "I don't know." In fairness, sometimes a person just feels poorly, and there is not an easily identifiable cause like a cold or backache. But at least try to verbalize what doesn't seem right to you and pinpoint when you first noticed it. Physicians will sometimes ask a patient what exactly they are feeling only to be given an even more obtuse answer like "That's for you to figure out." Inevitably, this will occur when you are running behind or just starting to catch up with your schedule. You cannot help but think to yourself, "You are not going to make this easy are you? A little cooperation might get us to an answer a whole lot faster."

Know why you have gone to the doctor, and try not to be vague, if you can help it. You will help yourself by helping your doctor help you. If we taught our children and adults how to be good patients, it would take considerably less time to provide better care. More patients could get to see their doctors, and people would waste less time sitting in waiting rooms because their doctor had been held up by such a patient. Patients could get in, out and on their way back to good health.

Office visit vs. urgent[88] vs. emergent[89] care

Health classes have failed to teach our citizens what is and is not an emergency. Too many people with urgent or emergent problems wait until their doctor's office opens or worse yet until the office secretary gives them an appointment. Far too many people, without urgent, let alone real emergencies, go to the emergency room for care. More than once while working in the ER, a person has come in requesting a Band-Aid for a small cut on his finger, insisting that he

---

[88] Injury or illness requiring immediate (same day) but not emergency care.
[89] Serious injury or illness requiring emergency room care.

had a right to treatment. In England, he would have been thrown out; here he will be seen. No country can afford this kind of access.

I will not attempt to go through a list of real emergencies here, but a good rule of thumb is anything that interferes with basic bodily functions, such as airway, breathing, circulation (heart beat/chest pain), for starters, or anything that causes an excessive loss of any bodily fluids from an orifice (natural or man-made), particularly the wrong bodily fluids (other than what would normally be expected), is an emergency.

While covering the emergency room at Deaconess Hospital in Cincinnati, a patient came in via squad with his family in what is referred to as agonal breathing, also known as the death rales or rattles.[90] As the name suggests, it is typical of the type of breathing that occurs close to death; the patient is not conscious of their environment at that point. I asked the patient's wife how long he had been like this. She answered a few hours. When a person is not breathing well and is not arousable, this should immediately indicate a problem. Our people do not need to be great diagnosticians to learn the basics of what is or is not an emergency. Our schools should be teaching this. Schools should also teach students how to find a family physician, how to make an appointment, and when to use an urgent care center[91] vs. an emergency room. Too many emergency rooms

---

[90] Merck Manual Home Edition: *When Death is Near*
http://www.merck.com/mmhe/sec01/ch008/ch008j.html [Accessed 6/20/09]
[91] "Urgent Care Centers are walk-in ambulatory care centers, generally open seven (7) days each week often 13 or more hours each day. No appointment is required for a patient to receive care. These centers have a broad array of diagnostic and therapeutic services, often including x-ray, laboratory testing, on-site pharmacy, procedure rooms for laceration and fracture care, exam rooms, and specialized corporate services for employee health and workers compensation cases." See http://www.urgentcare.org/FAQs/tabid/135/Default.aspx .

have beds tied up with non-emergency care, such as sinus infections, urinary tract infections, sexually transmitted diseases. In my experience, easily two-thirds of the care is non-emergent.

Access to care and the "lack" of it

So many times in this country we talk about a "lack of access to care." I do not believe most of those discussing the issue actually understand the true meaning of the phrase. The first week I was in Albania working at ABC Clinic in Tirana, a woman was brought in by her friend, her pastor, a church deacon and her young teenage daughter. She was apparently hemorrhaging and in disseminated intravascular coagulation (DIC). By the time she came into the clinic, she had lost a considerable amount of blood. We immediately ran some labs and started several large-bore IVs. The lab was around the corner and the doctor quickly got us the results. We had to get her to the hospital for care. Since there were no ambulances, the pastor, the deacon, the local Albanian doctor and I got the patient into the deacon's car, IV in tote, and drove over to the general hospital.

We saw the generalist, who called in the hematologist to look at the patient and go over the labs. They agreed with the diagnosis, but stated that she needed to go to the Women's Hospital for such problems. They did not handle such cases there. We piled back into the car and headed for the Women's Hospital. When we spoke to the head doctor at the Women's Hospital, he refused to admit her. Without examining her, he said she was fine, despite the fact that she could barely stand up on her own. I said the only reason she could even stand at all was because of the IV fluids we were giving her. He and the other doctors stood there laughing at us, as I pleaded with him to examine her, my Albanian colleague earnestly translating my pleadings. This patient would die in the next few hours if nothing was done. When the doctor chuckled and turned to leave, I seized hold of his forearm and told him, "She is going to die, and soon, if nothing is done and it will be on your head. Either help me or tell me where I can get her help." He tried to get away, but I wasn't letting go. It was then he looked me in the eye and said "Go to the Maternity Hospital." I thanked him and returned his arm.

When we got to the Maternity Hospital, the entrance was on the third floor. In the Third World, there is virtually never an elevator; and if there is one, it either hasn't worked in years, or there is no electricity. This particular hospital had no elevator. The two gentlemen with us carried our patient up three flights of stairs. When we got to the top, the heavy plate glass doors were locked. After beating on the door and waving my arms like a member of the ground crew at JFK bringing a plane into the gate, I finally got the attention of the doctors at the far end of the hall, who came, unlocked the door helped get the patient to an examining room, and took care of her. Now *this* patient had a lack of access to care on multiple levels.

When Americans refer to a lack of access to care, it is not usually this type of problem. It generally falls into one of three problems. The issue may be a lack of ability to pay for the treatment needed or fear of the lack of money to seek it. It may be that they live far from a local hospital. Unfortunately, on occasion in this country, a person will die in the waiting room of a hospital. It tends to happen when patients come to the ER themselves, rather than call an ambulance. This is due to insensitivity or the inability of the registration and ER staff to triage patients and prioritize care. It comes down to poorly managed resources, rather than a true lack of access to care.

Under the Emergency Medical Treatment and Active Labor Act (EMTALA) [Title 42 of the US Code, Chapter 7, Subchapter 18, Part E, § 1395dd]:

§ 1395dd. Examination and treatment for emergency medical conditions and women in labor
(a) Medical screening requirement
In the case of a hospital that has a hospital emergency department, if any individual (whether or not eligible for benefits under this subchapter) comes to the emergency department and a request is made on the individual's behalf for examination or treatment for a medical condition, the hospital must provide for an appropriate medical screening examination within the capability of the hospital's emergency department, including ancillary services routinely available to the emergency department, to determine whether or not an emergency medical condition (within the meaning of subsection (e)(1) of this section) exists.
(b) Necessary stabilizing treatment for emergency medical conditions and labor
(1) In general
If any individual (whether or not eligible for benefits under this subchapter) comes to a hospital and the hospital determines that the individual has an emergency medical condition, the hospital must provide either—
(A) within the staff and facilities available at the hospital, for such further medical examination and such treatment as may be required to stabilize the medical condition, or
(B) for transfer of the individual to another medical facility in accordance with subsection (c) of this section.[92]

---

[92]EMTALA http://www.law.cornell.edu/uscode/42/1395dd.html [Accessed 6/20/09]

As long as the patient is willing to consent to treatment, or transfer to a more appropriate facility should the hospital where he initially presented be unable to provide the necessary care, that patient will get emergency medical evaluation, stabilization and treatment.[93] There are well-defined processes and procedures regarding how transfers may take place and under what conditions. If these are not followed, the hospital and emergency room physician may each face civil monetary penalties under the federal law and may be subject to a personal injury suit by the patient under state law.

The Act specifically prohibits discrimination and delays in examining and treating patients due to insurance or the lack of it.

(g) Nondiscrimination
A participating hospital that has specialized capabilities or facilities (such as burn units, shock-trauma units, neonatal intensive care units, or (with respect to rural areas) regional referral centers as identified by the Secretary in regulation) shall not refuse to accept an appropriate transfer of an individual who requires such specialized capabilities or facilities if the hospital has the capacity to treat the individual.

(h) No delay in examination or treatment
A participating hospital may not delay provision of an appropriate medical screening examination required under subsection (a) of this section or further medical examination and treatment required under subsection (b) of this section in order to inquire about the

---

[93] "**(B)** The term "stabilized" means, with respect to an emergency medical condition described in paragraph (1)(A), that no material deterioration of the condition is likely, within reasonable medical probability, to result from or occur during the transfer of the individual from a facility, or, with respect to an emergency medical condition described in paragraph (1)(B), that the woman has delivered (including the placenta).
(4) The term "transfer" means the movement (including the discharge) of an individual outside a hospital's facilities at the direction of any person employed by (or affiliated or associated, directly or indirectly, with) the hospital, but does not include such a movement of an individual who **(A)** has been declared dead, or **(B)** leaves the facility without the permission of any such person [against medical advice]." See EMTALA definitions http://www.law.cornell.edu/uscode/42/1395dd.html [Accessed 6/20/09]

individual's method of payment or insurance status.

Unlike in virtually every other country in the world, where if you do not have a citizen identity card or a credit card in hand, you cannot receive treatment, we may have made it *too* easy to receive access to care.

Before you think that last statement preposterous, consider the findings of this study by Weinick, et al.:

> For those without a usual primary care provider or who cannot afford their services, the ED [emergency department] provides an attractive option: no one is turned away, no proof of income is required, and often no payment is required at the time services are delivered. In addition, Medicaid patients are more likely to utilize emergency departments in part due to difficulties accessing office-based physicians who are willing to accept Medicaid fees schedules.
>
> A substantial portion of visits to emergency departments are for non-urgent conditions which could be treated in primary care settings. These types of ED visits likely reflect poor primary care accessibility and many limitations of primary care discussed above...Cunningham et al. found that very young children were more likely to use the emergency department for non-urgent care – possibly related to parents' inability to reach their usual provider after regular office hours. Patients who utilize EDs for ambulatory care were more likely to report non-financial barriers to care, such as an inability to access evening services or get time off work, no timely clinic appointments, and failed attempts to get care elsewhere. One Canadian study reported that, among a largely insured cohort, 55 percent of patients utilized the emergency department for reasons of convenience. This and several other studies suggest that the more traditional hours of primary care physicians are leading patients to seek care when it is convenient for them.
>
> ..To better understand this use of EDs, the New York University Center for Health and Public Service Research and the United Hospital Fund of New York have developed and algorithm to profile ED use...Patients in the sample were classified as "Non-emergent"

if the initial complaint and vital signs indicated care was not required within 12 hours. Records of "emergent" patients (requiring care within 12 hours) were further examined to assess the resources used in the emergency department. Patients using no resources or resources typically available in a primary care setting were classified as "Emergent—Primary care treatable."… Computerized ED data was obtained for New York City hospitals for 1994 and 1998,… regarding ED usage in New York City.

- There is significant ED use for conditions that are non-emergent or that are emergent but could be treated in a primary care setting. For children age 0-17, 41.6% of ED use was for non-emergent conditions, with another 36% for emergent but primary care treatable conditions. Only 22.4% of use required ED services, and almost one-third of this use (7.6% of all use) was potentially preventable/avoidable with effective and timely primary care earlier in the episode of illness. For adults similar rates were observed, with 41.7% non-emergent and 32.4% emergent, but primary care treatable.
- The relative rates of non-emergent and primary care use differed by payer. Rates were highest among Medicaid children and lowest among commercial patients, with self pay /uninsured patients falling in between the two.
- Relative rates also differed by race/ethnicity and gender. Black and Hispanic/Latino patients had higher relative rates of use for non-emergent or primary care treatable conditions across all payer classes, and males had higher rates than females.[94]

End the frequent flier programs

Keep the airline programs in place, but let us end the ER frequent fliers. These are the patients who use the ER for primary or urgent care. Some come in as often as once or twice a week. These patients often have one or more chronic conditions that are poorly controlled. This is sometimes because they have a doctor that is hard to get an

---

[94] Weinick R, Billing J, Burstin H. What is the role of primary care in emergency department overcrowding? See http://www.kaisernetwork.org/health_cast/uploaded_files/WeinickED.pdf

appointment with, but most of the time it is because they have not refilled their medicines. Now they are coming in with sky-high blood pressure or blood sugar. This is a personal responsibility issue. A follow-up appointment should have been made for them by their doctors' office before their pills and refills ran out. Or the patient should have done it himself. If ER abuse is a pattern, public and private insurance should at most cover 20% of the visit, and let the patient cover the rest. The insurer's explanation of benefits statement, which states what has been paid and what the patient owes, should include a list of several in-network primary care and urgent care centers within a given radius of the patient for future reference.

Interestingly, the frequent fliers do not like to fly coach; they almost always fly first class. In healthcare, that means coming by ambulance. (Incidentally, that practice also ties up ambulances from getting to real emergencies.) They know that they will go to the front of the line, ahead of patients in the waiting room, deserved or not, and be put in an ER bay for evaluation. This is often nothing more than a $500 or more taxi ride. We all know the story of the little boy who cried "Wolf!" too often; [95] as a country, we cannot afford this. If it is not due to trauma or the patient is not admitted to the hospital, the bill should be the patient's responsibility. (A few exceptions may need to be delineated, but I trust you have grasped the point.)

We must teach our citizens how to be wise consumers of healthcare. Find out what services are available at the local urgent care clinics. Most offer x-rays, basic lab tests, electrocardiograms

---

[95] Aesop's Fables http://en.wikipedia.org/wiki/The_Boy_Who_Cried_Wolf [Accessed 6/20/09]

(EKGs), aerosol treatments, etc. Ask family, friends, co-workers and neighbors if they have a doctor they like, with convenient hours.

Taking responsibility for yourself

While we can debate whether healthcare is a right, good health is always a privilege. People in the Third World know this. When I was working in the former Soviet republics of Georgia and South Ossetia, a good wage was $25 to $30 per month. While surveying the people along the border region, trying to ascertain what people would consider a fair price for an office visit, I found that people were willing to pay $5 to $6 dollars. This was equivalent to one week's salary. They thought this was a fair price! They understand that if they are sick, there is no one who will bail them out. Social services exist on paper, but in reality there is no money to provide them. It is hard to get good healthcare, and they understand the privilege of being healthy. As my mother taught me, "With every privilege, there is a responsibility."

You ask, "How can I be more responsible?" Know what you have been diagnosed with after you go to the doctor, the urgent care center or the hospital. Read up on it. Go to reliable Internet sources, such as:

The Merck Manual Home Edition	http://www.merck.com/mmhe/index.html
The Centers for Disease Control	http://www.cdc.gov/
The National Institutes of Health	http://health.nih.gov/
NIH Clinical Trials	http://www.clinicaltrials.gov/
Cleveland Clinic	http://my.clevelandclinic.org/health/default.aspx
Mayo Clinic	http://www.mayoclinic.com/health/DiseasesIndex/DiseasesIndex

Do <u>not</u> go to sites like www.joeshealthcare.com (This is a fictitious site, but you understand the need to be discriminating in where you go for advice.) Know what medicines you have been given. Do you have a chronic, long-term, problem or is this an illness you are going to treat and be done with? It happens with alarming frequency that a patient will be started on an anti-hypertensive, blood pressure, medication, given a 30-day supply and show up in the emergency room 40 days later complaining of a splitting headache that he cannot get rid of. When questioning the patient, you will find that he saw his doctor about a month earlier. His blood pressure was found to be a little high. The patient was given a medication he cannot recall, took it and thought that would fix the situation. Ideally, the doctor should have taken the time to explain to the patient the nature of his new-onset and likely chronic condition, as well as what lifestyle choices he might make to improve the situation or prevent himself from getting worse. This conversation may or may not have occurred. Patients sometimes do not hear what they do not want to hear. On the other hand, doctors are human. Sometimes they are interrupted or distracted. Sometimes they must address a number of problems on that visit, and patient education may be overlooked or left until a follow-up visit. While there is no excuse for sloppiness, we are all human beings living in an imperfect world. Ultimately, we are responsible for our own health, which means learning about what we were diagnosed with and how it is being treated.

Whether through modeling good patient behavior in television shows or teaching students in the classroom, we must teach our citizens how to be educated patients and consumers of healthcare. An educated patient will make the most of his follow-up visit with his physician. He will be ready to discuss his lifestyle and what changes he might make, because he has put some effort into thinking about it before he gets to the doctor.

Bother to know what medicines you are taking, what their names are and for how long you need them. Ask if your condition will be cured with this 30-day supply of pills or is this something you may need to take for the rest of your life. Think about how you feel when you are taking them. Are they helping you? Do you feel any better? See if there is any noticeable improvement in your symptoms. I cannot tell you how many times a patient has asked for a refill of, for example, an allergy medication. When I asked if it was helping him, he said, "I don't know. The doctor said I needed it." Pay attention to the effects of a medicine on you, there are many treatment options if one medicine is not effective for you. If you have allergies, you should know at what times of the year you need to use your medication. You should know when you don't have symptoms, you don't need to take it. Also, let your doctor know what supplements you are taking. For some reason, when it is *natural*, as opposed to pharmaceutical, patients believe it can only do them good, forgetting that arsenic is natural too!

Sometimes even doctors who are patients will forget to mention another medication or supplement until they are home and about to take another pill. When this happens, call your doctor or pharmacist and ask if it is all right. If your pharmacy or doctor's office is closed, you can look it up on www.drugs.com . This site has a drug interactions checker that lets you put in your medications, supplements and even foods, such as grapefruit, that may interact with other medicines. *As the site's disclaimer says, it is not a substitute for your doctor or pharmacist, but it can alert you to potential problems.*

Until we have a nationally accessible electronic medical record, patients should ask their doctors for copies of any lab or diagnostic procedures and place them in a folder at home. (If you ask during your follow-up visit you won't be charged for them.) Many times, due to a lack of accessibility, tests are repeated. Sometimes this happens when a patient shows up at the hospital, seeks a second opinion or is referred to another specialist. This is often unnecessary and always costly. It may also be terribly inconvenient and uncomfortable for the patient depending on the issue at hand. When I was doing a clinical rotation in hematology and oncology at Allgemeines Krankenhaus[96] in Vienna, after making morning rounds and recording the test results in the chart, the head doctor gave a hard copy of the labs to the patient who put them in a manila folder in a bedside drawer.

Clearly, we can train our people to be just as responsible. They can bring their folders with them to appointments. They do need to make certain they get everything back from their doctors before they leave or only bring their doctors copies.

If your insurance company will not pre-certify a procedure, that may indicate one of four things: 1.) The office did not send medical records needed to demonstrate the symptoms and findings and that a complete workup was done. 2.) The workup was incomplete. 3.) Medical criteria indicating the need for a procedure or test were not met. 4.) It is not a service covered under the terms of the policy. You have the right to ask your insurer why the request was not pre-

---

[96] This is the national/state hospital for Austria and one of the top three medical centers in Europe.

certified.

If you have any doubts regarding any major procedure or the procedure seems rather radical, get a second opinion. That does not mean that you need another million-dollar workup to do so. Bring copies of the medical reports and any copies of radiology scans, most x-rays, CT and MRI scans can be put on a CD for you to bring to your consultation. The consulting physician may find a need to order additional tests, but the entire workup does not need to be repeated. Unless death is imminent, patients should do their homework and read up on their recommended procedure. Patients should seek a second opinion if they are less than confident about the options presented to them.

Take home message

After any visit, diagnostic or procedure, ask when you are to come back for follow-up. Don't leave things to chance. Never accept a statement like, "If you don't hear back from us about a given test, it is all right." Too many times inexperienced staff will file the results of a test before a doctor sees them, and you will not get them until the next time you go to the doctor which may be months if not years later, or at all, given the frequency with which patients relocate to other cities. Too much morbidity and mortality has been caused by such foolishness. While this practice has been largely abandoned by offices, on occasion I will still hear patients say that their physician's office give them the "no news is good news" line. On the contrary, no news is simply not any news. Ultimately, you are responsible for your health. You have a duty to yourself and those that depend on you to make certain you get the results of the medical services for which you and/or your insurer have paid.

Chapter 8

Better Quality = Less Liability

Addressing quality
—The role of state boards, medical educators and hospitals

A few years ago, I had the opportunity to give a presentation before the American Association of Osteopathic Examiners. This group consists of all of the osteopathic physicians who sit on state medical boards. Although my presentation was early in the day, I stayed to hear the rest. The discussion surrounded the issue of how to address problem physicians. Some practioners had been great physicians, but in whom colleagues noticed were now unfortunately declining in mental acuity. The issue was how to deal with these physicians gently without having to file formal actions against them with a state medical board. No one wanted to dishonor someone who had a lifetime of great service because he was now declining in function. I asked, "Shouldn't their partners, the chief of staff and a few appropriate colleagues sit down and have a conversation with those practitioners?" I was told that physicians were extremely reluctant to do so, perhaps in fear that one day they might be in the same situation. Aging in the workforce is a problem for anyone in a safety-sensitive position, and it will increasingly be so, as our country's demographics change. At some point, physical or mental abilities may make it impossible to do the job to the standards required. This should not be a shame, but there must be a mechanism to modify an aging physician's practice or retire the practitioner entirely without it becoming a public disgracing.

The conversation shifted to how to get outright bad practioners out of practice. The methods thus far have been continued testing, including board recertification every 7 to 10 years. The problem with that is that by the time doctors get through medical school they are professional test takers. I would venture to say that perhaps two or three members of any medical school class should never have become doctors in the first place. They may be able to memorize facts, but they have not a clue how to apply them to the patient in front of them.

Other physicians may have some serious personality disorder or be of questionable character for the medical profession. It is important to find out how they think and what motivates them. For example, you do not want someone recommending a treatment, because he is looking for a body to do a procedure on, as is increasingly the case. Nor do you want to have a doctor take advantage of a patient in a compromising position. Due to the expense, psychological testing is no longer required of applicants as it was in the past, despite the fact that it has proven quite effective as a screening mechanism. In his book, The Motivation to Work, Frederick Hertzberg, analyzed 200 Pittsburgh engineers and accountants for the factors that led to job satisfaction or dissatisfaction. His work became one of the most replicated studies in the field of workplace psychology, particularly in the area of hiring the right people for a job. By analyzing the work habits and personality traits of those who are already successful in a particular position, interview surveys specific to that job were reliably produced "to be used as a tool in placing the right person in the right job." Although no tool is perfect, such a screening device might eliminate a good number of bad physicians. Unfortunately, due to high tuitions[97] and legal concerns, it is virtually impossible to be expelled from medical school for any reason other than grades. The General Medical Council, which registers and licenses physicians in the U.K., wrote in a comprehensive paper, "Tomorrow's Doctors" that "Only those students who are fit to practice as doctors should be allowed to complete the curriculum and gain provisional registration. Students who do not meet the necessary standards in terms of demonstrating appropriate knowledge, skills, *attitudes* and *behavior* must be advised of alternative careers to follow."[98, 99]

Unfortunately, residency programs are no better in acknowledging a problem, even from within the system. This story illustrates many of the issues that may arise. While I was contracted to cover a hospital's employee health department in a major Ohio city, a first year resident was doing a procedure on a patient. He had a needle stick. In such instances, both the doctor and patient must be tested for blood-borne

---

[97] Medical school tuitions alone are now between $35,000 and $65,000 annually.
[98] Smith DA. *The Focal Point for the Next Generation.* Unpublished work, Registered © 2004.
[99] *Medical Students: Professional behavior and Fitness to Practice.* General Medical Council, 2007. [This delineates solid guidelines as to how to evaluate fitness to practice in doctors in training.]

pathogens. The nursing staff and I tried to explain this to no avail. He insisted that despite his laceration, he could not possibly have contaminated the patient. She contaminated him. It was "unscientific" to think otherwise. He was clearly the victim. He refused testing, despite my explaining the need and his ethical responsibility. Given the potential for cross-contamination, and that it was to his advantage to protect himself from liability. If she later contracted a blood-borne pathogen, he would have proof that he did not harbor such a pathogen at the time of the incident. He did not want to sign consent for treatment and voiced his unhappiness about signing *any* paperwork for Workers Compensation (WC), stating it would not pay him anything. I advised him of the importance of transparency in this matter and the need for him to be tested as well. Any perceived attempt on his part to cover up any illness he had by not getting tested would only make matters worse for him. He needed to own up to the fact that an accident had occurred, albeit inadvertently, and do the right thing so that any needed treatment could proceed as quickly as possible. As a former benefits administrator, I walked him through the mechanics of the WC system and the medical liability, both personally and for hospital systems. I explained my duty to do right by him, the patient and the hospital by following the protocols that have been established for such instances. Avoiding the protocols would open us up to unlimited liability. I explained to him that accidents happen, but we have to do everything possible to make things right after they do. It is essential that he be as concerned for the welfare of his patient as he is for himself. He continued blaming the patient for contaminating him. He insisted he was clean and disease-free. As a doctor, he believed he was above reproach, as evidenced by his even coming to Employee Health. When I voiced concerns about his apparent lack of medical ethics, he replied, "Those are *your* ethics, not mine. You have no right to judge me by them." I was about to respond that those are in keeping with the AMA guidelines and state law, but at that point he jumped up, swinging his arms wildly. He was ranting and raving, "That's why no one wants to come to Employee Health! You people only want to report and punish us for something that was an accident! I should have never come here…It was a big, big mistake! I'll never do that again. I shouldn't have said anything. I should have gone somewhere else and been checked out! I just wanted *her* to get tested!" He returned roughly an hour later, requesting testing, which was done.

Do you see the problems here?

a. Lack of respect for the rights of the patient as a human being.
b. Blaming the patient for *his* contamination of the procedure field.
c. Inability to take full responsibility and too immature to take appropriate actions.
d. Unwillingness to follow set hospital procedure for testing, without regard for personal or employer liability.
e. Expressed willingness to cover up any future incidents without professional regard.
f. Lack of sound medical judgment and "scientific-ness."
g. An arrogant attitude that physicians are above reproach.
h. Berating the entire staff of the Employee Health Department.
i. Disruptive behavior.
j. Lack of medical ethics and a double-standard for behavior.

Do you want this doctor treating you or your family? Lest you think me unsympathetic, I also received a needle stick in my first year of residency. I understand the anxiety, but it excuses nothing. We need people who can acknowledge a problem, and do the right thing anyway. Otherwise, they need to be thrown out of the program and reported to the state medical board and the National Practitioner Data Bank (NPDB).

What was most disturbing was the response from his residency and graduate medical education directors, who dismissed the entire incident as a "misunderstanding" due to the fact that English was his second language. (He spoke English quite plainly with us. If he did not speak English well, should he be practicing here?) A formal complaint was filed, by a board-certified physician on staff with an academic appointment as a clinical assistant professor at a medical school, enumerating the serious concerns about this young man. The complaint was whitewashed - very disappointing.

Lip service to quality assurance

No doubt you would agree that hospitals should monitor the quality of practice of the physicians at their facilities. In fact, most hospitals have a Director or Chief or VP of Quality. It sounds like they care. However, after peer-reviewing thousands of patient records, I am skeptical. When a problem was pointed out in the spirit of quality assurance and process improvement, not to deny them pay, there was not one collegial response. In fact, one well known academic medical center in Boston, the director of quality assurance (QA) had also been involved with treating the patient in question. He thought it was all right to peer-review his own case! Not too surprisingly, the three-page letter he sent back was a ranting tirade attempting to justify what he did, instead of actually treating the patient's real illness. No matter how diplomatically written, hospitals do not want to be informed of any problems. For some reason, they believe if they discipline the doctor, they are culpable, when in fact the opposite is true. When cases raise questions in internal QA review, the final determining peer-review should be done by outside reviewers in the same specialty. Many firms specialize in this type of work. Reviews should be from two different firms and the reviewer should speak to the physician to learn the logic behind his decision. Problems have occurred when all this is done in-house. In some cases, local colleagues from the same specialty who wanted to get rid of their competition sat on hospital committees judging disciplinary actions. In-house peer-review also pits even the friendliest colleagues in the same specialty against one another unnecessarily.

To have hospital discipline or state medical board action is an ominous thing on a physician's record. It may affect a person's ability to get malpractice insurance, which will affect or even eliminate the ability to earn a living. This may explain the reluctance to report problems. But if peer-review is truly independent and procedures are followed, this should not be an issue. The reality is hospitals are afraid of lawsuits and bad press in their communities. Depending on the issue, it may need to be heard by the state medical board.

State medical boards can only act on information they are given from the public, professionals or hospitals. Timely investigation is sometimes an issue, as is jurisdiction. One case, I am aware of involved a healthcare practitioner practicing outside of his scope of practice. He was a non-physician ordering and performing procedures that he was not trained to do. The medical board passed the case off to this fellow's professional board, but it made the decision not to make a decision on the matter because of political reasons. In my experience, few medical boards know how to work effectively with their state attorney general's office in these matters. The board has no authority to impose actions or penalties on those outside their profession, let alone civil or criminal charges. These two groups need to cultivate ties to work together effectively to protect the public from harm.

At present, the NPDB collects information on all U.S. providers regarding all state medical board and certain hospital disciplinary actions. The NPDB was established to stop "bad" practioners from moving to another state and setting up practice.

> As of December 2007, almost 50 percent of the hospitals in the U.S. had never reported a single privilege sanction to the NPDB. Prior to the opening of the NPDB in September 1990, the federal government estimated that 5,000 hospital clinical privilege reports would be submitted to the NPDB on an annual basis, while the health care industry estimated 10,000 reports per year. However, the average number of annual reports has been only 650 for the 17 years of the NPDB's existence, which is 1/8th of the government estimate and about 1/16th of the industry estimate.[100]

This would appear to suggest that facilities are not fully dealing with problem physicians.

---

[100] Levine A, Wolfe S. *Hospitals Drop the Ball on Physician Oversight: Failure of Hospitals to Discipline and Report Doctors Endangers Patients.* Public Citizen; May 27, 2009. http://www.citizen.org/documents/1873.pdf

Hospitals, medical educators and medical boards should never act capriciously. Policies need to be laid out and followed to protect public safety. With any organization, mistakes in judgment, application of policy, or a lack of information may occur, which initially leads to the wrong conclusions. There must also be a mechanism to see that mistakes are rectified. Currently, only the organization that filed the action can remove it from the NPDB. Some organizations never do, despite being overturned by a higher authority or in the courts.

Common quality issues

Having peer-reviewed thousands of claims, these are the issues doctors need to address in their medical practice to improve quality. These should be common sense, but common sense is not necessarily common. Following the adage of old Dr. Still, "treat the disease not the symptoms," these are a few common quality peeves:

1. Ignoring test results and thus diagnoses.
2. Mentioning test results, but doing nothing and still failing to officially diagnose the underlying problem.
3. Ignoring common side effects of drugs the patient is currently taking as a source of trouble and adding more drugs to treat symptoms.
4. Listing symptoms as final diagnoses, rather than working diagnoses, never getting to the real cause even at the second, third and fourth visit.
5. Not knowing when to call for reinforcements and get a specialist's opinion or as my professors said "Knowing when to punt."
6. Silo thinking by specialties, particularly in the hospital setting. Not seeing the forest for the trees.

7. Practicing "cover your behind" medicine.
8. Working up what the doctors want, rather than what the patient has.

Unfortunately, the last two items are highly correlated, especially in the ER these days. For example, one patient was an older fellow with a remote history of cardiac disease. His complaints were nausea and left flank pain, and he had nonspecific EKG changes. Despite three negative serial troponin blood tests, which would rule out 99% of cardiac causes, they proceeded with an echocardiogram. When that was negative, they performed an angiogram, which was also negative, and sent the patient home. Along the way someone thought to order a urinalysis, which indicated a pyelonephritis, a kidney infection. No physical examination was recorded of any organ system, let alone, of the heart, chest and abdomen. It seems the patient was not treated for his kidney infection. Hopefully, the patient received some symptomatic relief from the bag of IV fluids he received during his long ER stay. He was discharged with the name of a family practitioner to make an appointment in a week, if he did not feel better. Over $22,000 was spent, and this poor gentleman *did not even get treated for his problem*, which could have been diagnosed with a good physical examination, a few pertinent questions and a urine dipstick strip ($2 for the lab). After three negative serial troponins, no further cardiac workup was justified. This is "cover your behind" and make certain nothing awful is going on, then let the family practitioner figure it out if there is still a problem. It is not good medicine, and it has increasingly become a problem over the last two years. Frankly, if the doctor has not done a pertinent physical exam, he ought not be paid. He has not provided the patient with a service. This should be a big red flag. Negative serial troponins should also trigger a red flag (clinical and payment-wise), when additional cardiac tests continue to be ordered. A physician who insists on chasing down a path that has been clearly ruled out should be required by the director of QA to take some continuing medical education, and make a presentation on the diagnosis and treatment of the condition at a hospital morning or noon lecture. This should be a learning experience for everyone.

If local physicians correct and discipline their own, either formally or informally, and have the mechanisms in place to learn from their experiences, legal actions are less likely. Practitioners will know that they must be on their toes. When a problem is brought to light, the hospital, facility or medical practice should investigate it objectively, preferably with outside peer-review. If this is done expediently, the facility should have limited liability. If there is any cover-up or whitewashing, they have reason to be worried.

Working with the legal profession

Impossible as it may seem, the medical and legal professions can work together to improve the health and safety of the American people. Putting aside traditional adversarialism for a few moments, let us explore the idea.

First, we should work together on public health[101] and medical

---

[101] The term "public health" means the science and practice of protecting and improving the overall health of the community through disease prevention and early diagnosis, control of

preparedness,[102] particularly when bioterrorism and pandemic disease outbreaks are a very real threat to the health of our people. In its policies, the American Bar Association (ABA) states:

> …Encourages state, territorial and local bar associations to work with public health authorities to develop programs that train lawyers to provide pro bono legal assistance to public health authorities confronting biological and other health emergencies. Encourages ABA members and lawyers throughout the United States to become involved in assessing and improving the public health legal preparedness of the communities in which they live and work and ensuring that public health measures are protective of civil and constitutional rights. [103]

For the health and safety of the public, authorities may need to quarantine people who have been exposed to certain substances for continued monitoring and treatment or to prevent further contamination or drug-resistance in the community. People tend to think they have a right to do as they please. Those rights end when a person becomes a hazard to the public. For example, when patients infected with tuberculosis do not comply with treatment, they can as a last resort be "involuntarily detained" for several months until completion of directly observed treatment (someone watching them

communicable diseases, health education, injury prevention, sanitation, and protection from environmental hazards. http://www.dhs.gov/xabout/laws/gc_1219263961449.shtm [Accessed 6/20/09]

[102] The term "public health and medical preparedness" means the existence of plans, procedures, policies, training, and equipment necessary to maximize the ability to prevent, respond to, and recover from major events, including efforts that result in the capability to render an appropriate public health and medical response that will mitigate the effects of illness and injury, limit morbidity and mortality to the maximum extent possible, and sustain societal, economic, and political infrastructure.
http://www.dhs.gov/xabout/laws/gc_1219263961449.shtm [Accessed 6/20/09]
[103] American Bar Association's Policy on Legislative & National Issues
http://www.abanet.org/policy/Ch-13greenbook2008-09.pdf [Accessed 6/20/09]

take their pills).

The medical profession, particularly public health officials, should give continuing education lectures at local and state bar associations. The two groups should partner with the media for a series of stories on "Public Health & the Law." They could prepare joint public service announcements to run in the event of an emergency. Should a disaster occur, we will need everyone's cooperation and understanding to limit the extent of illness and casualties. This is a serious public safety issue; we need to educate the public.

We could also work together to develop well-written informed consent authorizations for medical procedures that we all agree an average, reasonable person can understand. Specialty colleges [both DO and MD] should collate and write up written consent forms for common procedures done by their specialists. This should be done in concert with the ABA. There is currently no standardization of these forms, even among specialists in the same specialty. These forms should have an easy-to-read, set format with respectfully written, plain language that your grandmother would understand—no legalese or medical jargon allowed. If both specialty colleges and the ABA signed off on them, they would become the standard.

There are many other areas in which we can work together to increase public safety, improve accessibility and better respect the wishes of patients. These include effective pain management, telemedicine licensure and portable medical orders, such as advanced directives. This last issue is a major one, as patients frequently do not discuss their wishes with their families. Their families come to the hospital insisting that doctors "do everything" even when that was not the patient's wish and it will not necessarily be of any benefit to the patient. In fact, it usually prolongs patient misery.

Understanding the limits of medicine

We need to educate our patients about reasonable expectations, given their condition. When I was about 14, a friend of the family was visiting and we found him collapsed in the yard, blue. A fellow doing work next door and I performed CPR, but our friend died at the hospital. A week earlier, he was visiting a friend who had been hospitalized for a heart attack, when he himself collapsed. He was evaluated at the time and told he had blockages of more than 90% in all major coronary arteries. He had not told his family of the incident. Nevertheless, I was quite upset. He was 58 years old and appeared to be the picture of health. My father, also a physician, told me, "Sometimes you do everything right, and the patient still dies." That is an important fact to recognize. A bad outcome is not necessarily malpractice. Everyone has to go sometime. It is not very nice. Not everything is amenable to treatment, as frustrating as that is.

Side effects from an appropriate medication or treatment are not malpractice, but failure to recognize and adjust for them is. Patients need to assist in this process by noticing how their body is or is not responding and reporting it to their doctors in a timely manner.

Complications of a procedure are just that. Not all patients respond to treatment. Not all anatomy looks like the textbook. Those needing a procedure may not always be in optimal condition for surgery.

Even with the best-written disclosures, no one should sign any paper they do not fully understand, particularly when giving permission to do something to his body. As a consumer, it is the patient's responsibility to ask questions until he understands. No question is stupid. If the doctor does not seem to have time, find another who will give you the information you need to make a decision.

Medical malpractice

No one wants to see patients harmed by bad medical practice or negligence, least of all doctors. The problem with the current civil system is that doctors are not judged by a jury of their peers; they are judged by non-medical people. (Anyone who has ever been in a meeting of physicians can verify that doctors tend to be the harshest critics of one another.) Both the plaintiff's and defendant's lawyers proceed to parade their experts in front of the medically naive jury. Between the few unscrupulous physicians who make an excellent living saying whatever will benefit the party paying them and good lawyers who divert attention from the actual medical issue, it is small wonder that the process is seen as less than fair.

The standard we use in the insurance industry is outside peer-review. Why not apply that to malpractice cases? A panel of say, five qualified, same-specialty physicians[104] vetted and appointed by the

---

[104] Peer-reviewers are board-certified and tend to have a number of years of clinical practice experience, as well as an academic appointment and/or research background. They are professionals who are authorities in their field. These individuals should not be from areas in close geographic proximity to the defendant, to avoid appearance of a conflict of interest.

state medical board could peer-review the medical records of the case. The plaintiff, defendant and their counsels and experts could make presentations before the panel and the panel could question both sides. Much like the Supreme Court, the panel would deliberate, vote and write an opinion, including dissenting views.

If the panel decides that there is a case, it would proceed to the courts. A jury of the general public would hear the case and then be given a copy of the panel's report. In the presence of the attorneys and judge, the jury could question a member representing the panel regarding the report. The member may not give an opinion. The opinion is the report. His job is merely clarification. The jury would then be sequestered to deliberate the case and judgment award.

There are two components to the award. "The term 'economic damages' refers to past and future monetary expenses of an injured party, such as medical bills, rehabilitation expenses, and lost wages. 'Noneconomic damages' refers primarily to damages for pain and suffering. Economic and noneconomic damages are both compensatory damages; i.e., they are intended to compensate the injured party. Punitive damages (also called exemplary damages), by contrast, are awarded not to compensate plaintiffs but to punish and deter particularly egregious conduct on the part of defendants— generally meaning reckless disregard for the safety of others, and more than negligence or even gross negligence. Punitive damages are noneconomic by nature, but state statutes that impose caps on punitive damages usually treat them separately from compensatory noneconomic damages."[105] Many advocate limiting noneconomic damages and punitive awards to $250,000. In most cases that is reasonable; however, I have also seen some horrific mistakes that $250,000 would not cover. Limits have been shown to decrease medical malpractice rates for physicians. However, I believe the solution just presented is fair to everyone, eliminating frivolous suits and moving only credible suits forward. Medical judgment is determined by same-specialty medical professionals who understand how to apply the standards of care to the case. The damages are determined by a jury representing the public, with the standard oversight by a trial judge.

Medical malpractice truly is eliminating "access to care" in many parts of the country. In West Virginia, I was told by a gentleman on the medical board at the time that virtually every suit brought, resulted in a judgment against the doctor. In fact, it had gotten so bad that certain specialties were in danger of becoming extinct in the state, such as trauma surgeons and neurosurgeons. Imagine if you or a loved one were in an accident with a head injury, and there was *nowhere in the state* you could be flown for treatment. A considerable number of states face this issue with "high risk" specialties, such as those listed above, as well as obstetricians, cardiothoracic surgeons and anesthesiology. Other physicians in high liability states have chosen to limit their scope of practice to reduce their liability.[106] Others move

---

[105] Congressional Research Report for Congress. *Medical Malpractice Liability Reform: Legal Issues and Fifty-State Survey of Caps on Punitive Damages and Noneconomic Damages, April 11, 2005.*
http://shelby.senate.gov/legislation/MedicalMalpractice.pdf
[106] Cassels, C. *Aggressive Malpractice Environments Dictate How, Not Where, Neurosurgeons Practice.* Medscape Conference Coverage, based on selected sessions at the:

to another state. We can no longer ignore this growing problem.

American Association of Neurological Surgeons (AANS) 76th Annual Meeting. Abstract 602.
April 28, 2008. http://www.medscape.com/viewarticle/573903

Chapter 9

Becoming better companies and employers

As employers face double-digit raises in premiums annually, many have begun to look for ways to improve the health of their employees. Executives are asking prospective insurers and disease management companies what products they have to get their employees in better shape, with better health habits and to get those employees with chronic diseases under better control.

The following story was related to me by the medical staff at one of the companies for which I worked. The corporate executives were up in arms because their healthcare costs were going through the roof. Let me give you a bit of background about this company[107] and the people in it. The average age of its employees was 54. Due to the nature of the business, the employees worked 10 to 12 hour days from late fall to spring. But they worked limited shifts once or twice a week during the warm months. The company is located in a small town just

---

[107] Conlin, M. *Get healthy – or else.* Business Week, February 26, 2007. http://www.businessweek.com/magazine/content/07_09/b4023001.htm?link_position=link1

outside of Columbus, OH, and many employees also had family farms. This work schedule was convenient for farming. While this company was a manufacturing plant, most of the jobs had been automated and did not require the physical work they once did. Farmers work hard, but they do most of their work in spurts. Most of it is done during spring planting and fall harvest. These employees were anything but lazy. They were salt-of-the-earth, hard-working Americans, trying to get ahead in the world, provide for their families and send their children to college. But despite working long hours, they were not getting enough physical activity for their bodies to consider it exercise. Nothing got their heart rates up. As a result, most employees were overweight enough to be considered medically obese. The average employee had been working for the company for well over 25 years; many considered their co-workers like extended family. Due to the long hours and friendly environment, it was not unusual for employees to bring in casserole dishes to eat during their shift breaks. Typical of any manufacturing facility, workers were given smoke breaks and provided with vending machines in the break area.

This is a good company with good workers, many of them at risk for or diagnosed with metabolic syndrome[108] and similar health problems. The healthcare costs for its employees were eating into

---

[108] The 2001 National Cholesterol Education Program Adult Treatment Panel guidelines state that an individual with any three of the following traits meets the criteria for the metabolic syndrome: 1. Abdominal obesity defined as a waist circumference over 102 cm (40 in) in men and over 88 cm (35 inches) in women. 2. Serum triglycerides equal to or greater than 150 mg/dl. 3. HDL cholesterol of 40mg/dl or lower in men and 50mg/dl or lower in women. 4. Blood pressure of 130/85 or higher. 5. Fasting blood glucose of 100 mg/dl or greater.

20% of profits and growing at double-digit rates annually. Corporate executives were in a long meeting wringing their hands trying to figure out what could be done. In sheer exasperation, one executive said, "Let's just fire the fatties!" The other execs said that was not the answer. They agreed, "We have to come up with a better plan" and seriously set about to find a way to do that. The CEO even solicited employee feedback regarding how to make it easier for employees to get fit and stay healthy.

The company was determined to promote fitness. Overweight employees were encouraged to lose weight or pay the difference in premiums for their healthcare themselves. Smokers were given counseling and their choice of smoking-cessation tools, such as nicotine patches, Nicorette gum, or hypnosis, free of charge. Not only was the campus declared smoke-free, the executives were determined that all of their employees would be smoke-free as well, even in their off time. They conducted random periodic testing of employees who claimed they had quit. If they said they quit and had not, it would mean immediate dismissal. This might seem severe, but the company also invested $5 million in the health of its employees. It built a gorgeous fitness facility and medical clinic at the entrance of their manufacturing facility. A third-party company was brought in to manage the clinic and fitness facility, and ensure confidentiality. The fitness facility was staffed with physical therapists and personal trainers. Employees could receive medical care at the clinic, which had physicians, nurses and a nutritionist. Employees had to answer a health risk assessment questionnaire or pay $40 more per month for their healthcare costs. A full-time disease management nurse would counsel and follow-up with employee-patients who were deemed to be at high risk, either by the health assessment questionnaire or the clinic physicians. The nurse would provide patient education for employees in how to make proper lifestyle changes.

A corporate culture of health and fitness began to take hold, as employees became better educated about their health. Snack machines were now stocked with healthy choices and beverages. The high-fat, cheesy casseroles were replaced by healthier, low-calorie dishes, and new, tasty recipes were exchanged. Smoke breaks were replaced by walk breaks or fitness breaks.

By the time I was there, the program had been in place for several months. At first glance, it appeared to be an extreme wellness program. It was most certainly the right thing to do. As a public health physician, I was incredibly curious how this program was being received. A number of determined employees had already lost as much 75 to 100 pounds. In general, employees were getting fitter. They began to notice health changes in their co-workers, complimenting one another on their progress, as the wellness program instructed. If an employee was tempted to eat the wrong thing, their co-workers would encourage them to keep up the good work they had begun. Employees began to form fitness partnerships and work-out groups. A culture of positive peer pressure and encouragement took hold. When I spoke to patients, their response to this program was invariably the same, "I knew I needed to make some changes before this, but I was busy and just kept putting it off. This was just what I needed to make it happen."

Not every company can invest that kind of money into a wellness program, but companies should do the best they can where they are with what they have. Cover smoking cessation programs under your health plan. Change smoke breaks to fitness breaks. In many companies, and especially the military, it is all right to take a smoke break, but not all right to take break from the work at hand and take a quick walk around the block. It has been proven that a short break will help an employee to better focus when he returns to his job. Illogical as it seems, bosses have allowed for addictions, but not fitness and clarity of mind. Let's re-evaluate this process.

When evaluating various insurance plans, companies should ask insurers what disease management programs are available for high-risk employees. The depth of the programs, as well as the prices, vary considerably, and are not necessarily directly correlated. It pays to shop around.

A special note to self-insured employers

Those companies that are large enough to self-insure for healthcare need to monitor their third party administrators (TPAs).[109] Most provide good utilization review[110] services and process claims in a timely manner, but few have the skills needed to audit hospital bills specifically for errors and overcharges, particularly after a large hospitalization. Most TPAs use the summary of hospital charges[111] by

---

[109] Third party administrators handle the medical claims for companies which choose to self-insure for healthcare.
[110] Utilization review evaluates medical services for appropriateness and medical necessity.
[111] This is the CMS-1450 or the UB-92 Form.

broad revenue codes[112] in paying the claim, rather than doing a line item audit.

Stating eloquently in testimony before the Securities Exchange Commission, Mr. Jeff Barber, the vice president of a hospital bill auditing firm, verified that:

> In essence, the TPA is an external Accounts Payable Department for healthcare [for the employer]. In order to comply with privacy issues legislated under HIPAA; the TPA operates with little or no oversight by the corporation's internal auditors or outside CPA. There is a common misconception (even among Audit Committee members) that TPAs verify the accuracy and validity of employee healthcare bills, prior to paying claims. In actuality, TPAs and Preferred Provider Networks do not have the time, resources, expertise, or contractual obligation to confirm the accuracy of specific line-item charges. Most TPAs pay employees' hospital expenses from summary bills ("UB-92s"), which provide no itemization of charges. These simple invoices list charges by department only (Operating Room, Radiology, etc.), much like the first few pages of a phone bill. The difference? A phone bill provides several pages of detail, indicating every single call that is incorporated into the "balance due." Unfortunately, no such detail exists on a UB-92. Example: A hospital might charge a self-funded corporation $38,329.50 for medications described only as "Drugs-Generic." The summary bill would not specify the names of the medications, the quantities provided, or the unit pricing. Under the current system, it is impossible to verify the accuracy of employee benefit hospital bills. As a result, publicly traded corporate health plans routinely pay for:
> a) Hospital services that have not been provided;
> b) Hospital services that have been charged at an inflated rate. [113]

"According to a CMS study of 160,000 Medicare hospital bills; the average bill contains overcharges ranging from 5.6% in some

---

[112] Revenue codes are general classifications for payment such as laboratory, pathology, radiology, etc.

[113] Barber, J. *File NO. 4-511, Internal Control Roundtable (Sarbanes-Oxley Section 404)*. Security Exchange Commission Web site http://www.sec.gov/news/press/4-511/jwbarber2738.pdf

states to over 26% in others. (We have found the percentage of overcharges to be even <u>higher</u> in bills submitted to corporate health plans than in those submitted to the Medicare program.)"[114]

If your company is receiving a large bill, it may be worth getting a line-item audit, which requires matching the charges to the medical records.[115] If your TPA claims to be providing this service, it is not a bad idea to periodically have an outside hospital bill auditing firm check the quality of the work.[116] This is especially true given that multiple studies have shown that at least 90% of hospital bills contain errors,[117] with greater than 85% of them in favor of the hospital.[118] The old phrase, "let the buyer beware" applies here.

[114] Ibid.

[115] When I was working for a company that provided disease management services, it was recommended that all bills over $50,000 undergo a line item audit, as the minimum savings was at least 12%.

[116] *Medical-Bill Errors Increasingly Common.* Associated Press, October 28, 2007. http://www.hss.state.ak.us/dsds/docs/medicalBillErrors_APstory.pdf

[117] Rosenthal, Elisabeth. *The Problems: The Alert Consumer; Confusion, Errors and Fraud in Medical Bills.* New York Times, November 14, 1993. http://www.nytimes.com/1993/11/14/us/the-problems-the-alert-consumer-confusion-errors-and-fraud-in-medical-bills.html

[118] Akeso Care Management Web site http://www.akesocare.com/UnAuth/Services/ClaimReview.aspx [Accessed 6/20/09]

Chapter 10

Big pharma & medical device companies —Love the cure, hate the company

Americans have a strange love-hate relationship with big pharma and medical device companies. Initially, we hear of a discovery that looks like it will effectively treat or cure Disease X, and we eagerly wait for it to become commercially available, because so many people will benefit. Unfortunately, these new technologies and discoveries virtually never cost us less than previous treatment. This is justified by the fact that there either was no previous effective treatment or that this one is so much more superior that it cannot be compared.

According to the research, developing a new drug costs $802 million (2000 dollars)[119] and 12 years.[120] This figure has been disputed by some as overestimating the true expenses so drug companies can justify the costliness of the new medicines.

---

[119] DiMasi JA, Hansen RW, Grabowski HG. *The price of innovation: new estimates of drug development costs.* Journal of Health Economics 22 (2003) 151–185. http://www.cptech.org/ip/health/econ/dimasi2003.pdf [Accessed 6/8/09]
[120] *A Congressional Budget Office Study: Research and Development in the Pharmaceutical Industry.* October 2006; Pub. No.2589 http://www.cbo.gov/ftpdocs/76xx/doc7615/10-02-DrugR-D.pdf

While we understand the great undertaking needed to come up with a paradigm shifting innovation, the question remains: How come drugs are so much cheaper in other First World countries?

Having personally had such an experience while in France, I ran out of an antibiotic and was not quite over the infection I had. I went to the pharmacy to get a refill. The same medication that cost me $132 in Atlanta cost me $16 in France. Since I was there for the annual meeting of the World Health Assembly in Geneva and going to a reception sponsored by the International Federation of Pharmaceutical Manufacturers and Associations, I thought I might find out why there was such a discrepancy in price. I was told that it was in part due to the litigious nature of doing business in America. The costs of potential litigation are spread across the entire product line of a company and thus passed on to American consumers. It was also because the regulatory requirements of the Food and Drug Administration (FDA) were so onerous that it cost more to sell a drug in the United States.

Let's look at the first argument, as it bears some merit. It seems successful pharmaceutical products, even ones that have been on the market for years, often become the targets of a class-action lawsuits. The latest of these is Fleet® Phospho-soda® which has been on the market for 14 years as a bowel preparation for various diagnostic procedures. C.B. Fleet Company was formed in 1869. The first Fleet laxative was developed in 1893, and the first Fleet enema product was marketed in 1953. This is a well-established company with perceived deep pockets. As soon as the FDA put out a black box warning on the product and made it prescription only, the lawyers began circling.

C.B. Fleet Company immediately announced a voluntary recall of both their over-the-counter products Fleet® Phospho-soda® and Fleet® Phospho-soda® EZ-Prep® Bowel Cleansing System.

Why is FDA now recommending new steps for the safe use of these products when they have been used for years?

The FDA has received adverse event reports of acute phosphate nephropathy associated with the use of OSP [oral sodium phosphate] products. In 2006, FDA posted web information and a Science Paper describing reports of acute phosphate nephropathy associated with the use of prescription and over-the-counter OSP products. More recently there have been new reports of acute phosphate nephropathy with use of a tablet form of OSPs, Visicol.[121]

These products have been used by millions of people safely. However, with a greater pool of users, there are bound to be complications or side effects among certain subgroups. The reality is that despite all the testing that goes into obtaining FDA approval, not every possible subgroup and combination of races, sexes and age groups, with every combination of comorbidities and possible treatment combinations options can be tested. Virtually thousands of combinations would need to be sampled, in numbers great enough to be statistically useful. No drug would ever be approved if this were the case. Instead we try to get a smattering of the representative general population and the likely characteristics of the target group, including their likely comorbidities and medications. That does not mean every possible combination will be tried, but a good faith effort

---

[121] FDA Web site reference for OSPs [Accessed 6/20/09]
http://www.fda.gov/Drugs/DrugSafety/PostmarketDrugSafetyInformationforPatientsandProviders/ucm103383.htm

is made to obtain a representative sample. It seems highly likely that with general population usage, over time any product is likely to be found to have side effects or drug interactions in some sub-group.

The FDA approval process should mean something—that a good faith effort was put forth to ensure both safety and efficacy. This should provide full legal protection to the company and prevent future lawsuits, as more information becomes available and restrictions are placed on usage. "The average number of trials preformed to support approval of a new drug is currently more than fifty!"[122] It should also be noted that most drug studies are not done in the United States, due to the high costs. This is problematic because different ethnic groups may metabolize drugs differently. A good deal of testing is done in the developing world, where access to medications is limited as are drug interactions, for good or bad. While it may be good to get clear data about side effects and contraindications due to the drug itself, we will not so easily discover drug interactions, particularly with treatments for common comorbidities. This is why after-market testing is so important. This is where those black box labels and subsequent class action suits come into play. Given that the population is aging, with more comorbidities, contraindications, side effects and interactions are bound to be discovered. Realistically, that is all that can be reasonably expected. As new information comes in to the company and FDA that might suggest a problem, depending on the nature of that information, further action should be taken. If additional studies

---

[122] Miller, HI. *Failed FDA Reform*. Regulation; vol 21(3) 1998; 24-30. Reproduced with permission of the Cato Institute in the format Tradebook via Copyright Clearance Center. http://www.cato.org/pubs/regulation/regv21n3/v21n3-ftr2.pdf

need to be undertaken, study design and monitoring should occur under the watchful eye of the FDA. Any attempt to suppress adverse reports suggesting a problem would imply malicious intent; that would open a company to unlimited liability.

Protection of intellectual property has been criticized as keeping drug and medical device costs high. Why should a company spend $802 million to develop anything if it is going to be "open source"? It would seem companies are being asked to bear all the risk and expense, yet forfeit the reward early, which hardly fits the American dream in business.

We know that a company must make a profit in order to stay in business. It is projected that in order to commercialize a new molecular entity (NME), a company must make at least $500 million annually at its peak.[123] Drugs for more obscure diseases are less likely to be developed because they cannot, by nature of sheer numbers of ill people, reach the magic $500 million figure. The latest trend in pharmaceuticals is personalized medicines. That means the drugs you receive to treat a disease will be prescribed because, in you, that disease exhibits certain biomarkers. We will know exactly which drug will or won't work, in your specific case. We need to retool the drug development process so companies can bring a drug to market for a fraction of that $802 million, while taking all reasonable steps to maintain public safety. With lower peak annual sales required, more cures can be commercialized.

This requires a complete overhaul of the drug approval process.

---

[123] Rawlins, MD. *Cutting the cost of drug development.* Nature Reviews Drug Discovery 3, 360-364 (April 2004). http://www.stanford.edu/class/cbio101/coursework/rawlins2004.pdf

This cannot be a continued justification of the present processes, but rather a comparative examination of those processes vs. other First World countries.

> In 1973, the President's Science Advisory Committee concluded that it might be worth adapting US regulations so that not even a single important new entity introduced into selected foreign countries during the previous year fails to become available in the US." In 1976 the President's Biomedical Panel concluded that delays and costs that the FDA's protective systems impose on drug development constitute a "hazard to public health" But the FDA's policies and procedures were to become progressively more intrusive and expensive for drug manufacturers and patients alike. President Bush's Council on Competitiveness induced the FDA to announce various reforms in 1991, but the agency studied many of them literally to death, and turned its bureaucratic talents toward vitiating the others in a variety of ways…

> Section 903(b) of the law changes the FDA's mission, adding the obligation for "promptly and efficiently reviewing clinical research and making decisions "in a timely manner." But it is naive to think that this symbolism will have any effect on the agency's tradition of risk-aversion and foot-dragging. This section as well as section 803 (c)(3) requires the FDA to meet with foreign governments and to participate in efforts at international harmonization of regulation. However, the level of commitment to these efforts is reflected in the comment of one high ranking European official, in response to this author's enquiry about the progress of negotiations with the FDA on European-Unites States reciprocal drug approvals, "It's like discussing the Thanksgiving menu with the turkeys."[124]

Let us see where more efficiencies can be gained in the approval process. Typically, the FDA has claimed their delays in drug approval are due to a lack of staff. Application fees should cover the cost of each stage of evaluating the application.

---

[124] Miller, HI. *Failed FDA Reform*. Regulation; Vol 21(3) 1998; 24-30. Reproduced with permission of the Cato Institute in the format Tradebook via Copyright Clearance Center. http://www.cato.org/pubs/regulation/regv21n3/v21n3-ftr2.pdf

As an economist, I am not generally in favor of price controls or limits on a percentage of profits, as the former creates market distortions and the latter punishes efficiency in production. However, when certain drugs cost more than the median price of the average American home, it is inexcusable. The story behind one such overpriced drug was covered in the New York Times:

> Doctors are excited about the prospect of Avastin, a drug already widely used for colon cancer, as a crucial new treatment for breast and lung cancer. But many are cringing at the price the maker, Genentech, plans to charge for it: about $100,000 a year... With colon cancer, a year of Avastin treatment costs about $50,000. But the drug will be used at higher doses for lung and breast cancer, and Genentech does not plan to reduce the unit price, even though the additional cost of producing a higher dose is minimal. Because Genentech is a leading developer of cancer therapies, some doctors also fear that the company's pricing plans for Avastin around $8,800 a month may encourage other companies to charge more for their own oncology drugs. That could potentially drive up the overall cost of cancer treatment to unsustainable levels, they say.
>
> Right now, one of the few cancer drugs with a higher monthly price than the level planned for Avastin is Erbitux. The drug, used for colon cancer, sells for $9,600 monthly but is not as widely prescribed as Avastin and is typically used only as a last-resort treatment for a few months. Dr. Susan Desmond-Hellmann, the president of product development of Genentech, which is based in California, said the company had set Avastin's price based on "the value of innovation, and the value of new therapies."[125]
>
> Even some patients with medical insurance are hesitating before agreeing to the treatment, doctors say, because out-of-pocket co-payments for the drug could easily run $10,000 to $20,000 a year.

---

[125] Berenson, A. *A Cancer Drug Shows Promise, at a Price That Many Can't Pay*. From The New York Times, February 15, © 2009 The New York Times All rights reserved. Used by permission and protected by the Copyright Laws of the United States. The printing, copying, redistribution, or retransmission of the Material without express written permission is prohibited.
http://www.nytimes.com/2006/02/15/business/15drug.html?_r=1&sq=Berenson_february_2006&st=cse&scp=2&pagewanted=print

Until now, drug makers have typically defended high prices by noting the cost of developing new medicines. But executives at Genentech and its majority owner, Roche, are now using a separate argument citing the inherent value of life-sustaining therapies. If society wants the benefits, they say, it must be ready to spend more for treatments like Avastin and another of the company's cancer drugs, Herceptin, which sells for $40,000 a year. *"As we look at Avastin and Herceptin pricing, right now the health economics hold up, and therefore I don't see any reason to be touching them,"* said William Burns, the chief executive of Roche's pharmaceutical division and a member of Genentech's board. *"The pressure on society to use strong and good products is there."*[126]

"The pressure on society to use" —Is this guy serious? Who does he think he is kidding? This is an old fashioned "stick-up." This attitude needs to go. While we appreciate the value of innovation, we do not expect to be robbed.

With the emergence of the biologics in the pharmaceutical industry, diseases that were not previously "catastrophic" are now, due to the costs of these new treatments. For example, rheumatoid arthritis requiring Humira, Embrel or Orencia will cost around $20,000 per year to treat—for life.[127] (Ever wondered how they paid for all those ads on primetime TV?) Remember, this is *not* a cure, only a treatment.

If it truly costs $802 million for a NME, drug companies cannot expect to recover all their costs in two years. With a streamlined drug approval process and new legal protection under the FDA approval system, drug prices in the United States should resemble those of

---

[126] Ibid.

[127] Rucker, NL. *Biologics in Perspective: Expanded Clinical Options amid Greater Cost Scrutiny: Research Report.* AARP Public Policy Institute , June 2007. http://www.aarp.org/research/health/drugs/fs136_biologics.html

other First World countries. If drug companies will not lower prices on their own, then the government, the medical profession and the media should hold them accountable.

The physician's role

Physicians have unwittingly contributed to high drug expenditures by the American public. One very astute physician I had the pleasure of training with said, "You must read books. Your library must be current. No one can keep up with journal articles. The standard of care is in books. And above all, do not get your medical education from drug representatives. You must know what the standard of care is, including the drugs of choice for a patient with a given condition." Unfortunately many physicians do get their continuing pharmacology education from drug reps or drug-sponsored lectures. Most have not been trained to evaluate a medical study. Therefore, they may not know the right questions to ask. Rather than rely on research and convention, doctors must apply the *golden standard* of clinically-effective, cost-effective medicine.

The patient's role

Patients have also contributed to escalating drug expenditures in this country. This was not the case prior to direct-to-consumer marketing. Count how many pharmaceutical commercials you see in primetime television, especially for high-cost drugs such as Cialis, Viagra or Boniva. Pharmaceutical companies know patients will request the advertised drug. Doctors, in turn, will tend to give it to them if appropriate, rather than another drug or a lower cost alternative. Doctors want happy customers too. Frankly, this type of marketing is inappropriate for anything other than vaccinations, which have public health implications for the entire population, as opposed to an individual whim.

Patients would serve themselves well to pick up a list of the $4 per script drugs at a Wal-mart or Target, for example, and ask their doctors if one of them will work for their ailment. When patients do need a higher cost drug, they would also serve themselves well if they called a few local pharmacies and asked the price for filling the prescription. You may be surprised to find considerable variance. It is not unusual to see $30 or more. Connecticut, Florida, Maryland, Michigan, Minnesota, Missouri, New Hampshire, New Jersey, New York and Vermont have started Web sites for pharmacy price comparison, but they've drawn mixed reviews due to limited or outdated information.[128] It's worth checking to see what is available online; it is certainly worth a few phone calls. Most patients would rather not throw money away.

The role of FDA

When I was working at the CDC, it was well-known that the FDA was the most dysfunctional agency in government. "Since the 1960s the total time required for drug development—from synthesis in the

---

[128]Johnson, LA. *Drug Cost Comparison Web Sites Criticized.* Associated Press, February 14, 2008. http://www.usatoday.com/tech/products/2008-02-13-2375234124_x.htm

laboratory to the patient's bedside—has almost doubled from 8.1 years to 15.2 years."[129] Regulatory reform in the 1990s did little to positively impact the agency. Attempts to speed the introduction of generic drugs, as well as the transfer of drugs from prescription to over-the-counter use, have caused their own problems.

Making drugs more accessible—OTC is not always helpful

Patients want drugs to be available OTC because they no longer have to trouble themselves with a doctor's visit and copayment to obtain a refill. Employers and health plans like OTC medications because they are not covered under most plans, shifting the cost to the patient. This is particularly true for drugs like Zantac, Tagamet, Nexium, and Prilosec.

Historically, a shift to OTC usage has not been without problems, even for some drugs that were previously considered safe while they were prescription only. "There is no organized system for reporting the side effects of OTC drugs. Consequently, the FDA and drug manufacturers have virtually no way of knowing how common or serious the side effects are."[130]

A good example of this was the drug phenylpropanolamine (PPA). First formulated in 1910, this drug was a popular decongestant and safely used for decades while prescription only. It had an interesting

---

[129] Miller, HI. *Failed FDA Reform.* Regulation; Vol 21(3) 1998; 24-30. Reproduced with permission of the Cato Institute in the format Tradebook via Copyright Clearance Center. http://www.cato.org/pubs/regulation/regv21n3/v21n3-ftr2.pdf

[130] The Merck Manual Home Edition, edited by Robert Porter, M.D. Available at: http://www.merck.com/mmhe/sec02/ch018/ch018a.html. [Accessed 6/6/09].

and useful side effect in that it was also an appetite suppressant, and it had an indication as a weight-loss drug. Like most decongestants, it caused a rise in blood pressure. It had relatively tight dosing tolerances for safety, but it was used relatively safely when given under a doctor's guidance. When this drug was made OTC, 200 to 500 hemorrhagic strokes a year were suddenly occurring in young women aged 18 to 49. Being from a medical family, I was taught a healthy respect for medications, but I had a friend in high school who said, "If one is good, three is better." I believe a lot of people used the same rationale, particularly young women who want to lose weight. The risk of stroke was three times greater for women whose first usage of PPA was within 24 hours. Women who used the drug as an appetite suppressant were 16 times as likely to have a stroke in the first three days.[131] Some drugs should never be made OTC without a physical evaluation, particularly when they have potential for abuse. The FDA asked for a voluntary recall of all products in 2000 and completely banned sales in the United States in 2005. However, it is still sold safely in Europe by prescription only.

Patients will also tell their doctors, they have tried the OTC version of a drug, and it did not work. An example of this is the histamine (H2) blocker drugs like Zantac (ranitidine) and Tagamet (cimetadine), which worked quite well for most people with gastroesophageal reflux disease (GERD) previously. But, at one-quarter to one-half the prescription doses, the OTC version tends to be

---

[131] FDA Memorandum RE: Review of study protocol, final study report and raw data regarding the incidence of hemorrhagic stroke associated with the use of phenylpropanolamine. September 27, 2000.
http://www.fda.gov/ohrms/dockets/ac/00/backgrd/3647b1b_tab01.doc [Accessed 6/20/09]

subtherapeutic for all but the mildest cases. Doctors do not question

the dosage or frequency used, and naively proceed to go to higher

cost, proton pump inhibitors (PPI) like Prilosec (omeprazole) and

Nexium (esomeprazole magnesium). These PPI drugs have only had

controlled tests for six months of use,[132] yet many continue on them

for years.[133] The H2 blockers decrease gastric acid levels, and PPI

drugs are so effective that they block the production of virtually all

stomach acid, making it achlorhydric, inhibiting the absorption of

B12. Vitamin B12 is used in DNA synthesis and regulation

throughout the body. A B12 deficiency can cause depression and

difficulty in concentration in its mild state. When severe, it may cause

permanent damage to the brain and nervous system. Because patients

have a familiarity with these drugs, they do not appreciate the

potential long term consequences if left unmonitored. Nor do they

recognize the long list of potential interactions for these drugs, since

only a few are listed on the back of the container, with the caveat to

discuss the medication with your doctor.

The Merck Manual Home Edition describes the issue as such:

> ...all drugs have benefits and risks, and some degree of risk has to
> be tolerated if people are to receive a drug's benefits. Defining an
> acceptable degree of risk is a judgment call. Safety depends on
> using a drug properly. For OTC drugs, proper use often relies on

[132] Nexium Web site http://www.nexium-us.com/nexium-affordability/index.aspx [Accessed 6/6/09]

[133] Interestingly since the advent of these extremely effective drugs, the practice of medicine seems to have changed. Where if a doctor had previously prescribed an H2 blocker, before considering a PPI drug, he would order a GI consult for an EGD with biopsy to check for the bacteria H. Pylori and/or possible gastrinoma, a tumor in the duodenum or pancreas causing the hypersecretion of gastrin leading to increased stomach acid production. The GI doctor might order an MRI if he was suspecting the latter. Just getting rid of the acid does not get rid of the bacteria and it may mask early detection, and therefore treatment, of a tumor.

consumer self-diagnosis, which leaves room for error. For example, most headaches are not dangerous, but in rare cases, a headache is an early warning of a brain tumor or hemorrhage. Similarly, what seems like severe heartburn may signal an impending heart attack. Ultimately, people must use common sense in determining when a symptom or ailment is minor and when it requires medical attention and consult a doctor if they are unsure.

People who purchase OTC drugs should read and follow the instructions carefully. Because different formulations—such as immediate-release and controlled-release (slow-release) formulations—may have the same brand name, the label should be checked each time a product is purchased, and the dosage should be noted. Assuming that the dosage is the same is not safe. Also, different formulations with the same brand name may have different ingredients, so checking the ingredients on the label is important…When selecting a product, people should read the label carefully to determine which product is most appropriate for their particular problem. Labels on OTC drugs, which are required by the FDA, can help people understand a drug's benefits and risks as well as how to use the drug correctly. People should ask a pharmacist if they have any questions about an OTC product.

Often, the labels of OTC drugs do not list the full range of possible side effects. As a result, many people assume that these drugs have few, if any, side effects. For example, the package insert for one analgesic cautions people not to take the drug for more than 10 days for pain. However, the possible serious side effects that can occur with long-term use (such as life-threatening bleeding from the digestive tract) are not mentioned—not on the box, bottle, or package insert. Consequently, people with chronic pain or inflammation may take the drug for a long time without realizing that such use could lead to serious problems.[134]

Generic is not necessarily all it is cracked up to be

For the most part generic drugs are as good as their brand name

---

[134] The Merck Manual Home Edition, edited by Robert Porter, M.D. Available at: http://www.merck.com/mmhe/sec02/ch018/ch018a.html. [Accessed 6/6/09].

counterparts. However, what the public and even most physicians[135] do not know is that the FDA does not require identical bioequivalence. In fact, the variance may be anywhere between 80% and 125% of the brand name drug.[136] Too much leeway has been given unnecessarily. Is there any incentive for drug manufacturers to put too much medicine in a pill? Would this not be giving away their profits? It would seem that there is more incentive to put less in the pill, since the FDA permits it. While this may be less critical for antibiotics, it can seriously affect dosing for thyroid replacement and cardiac drugs. The dosing problem may be compounded if the patient used another pharmacy to fill the second prescription, which purchases their generics from another manufacturer. No more than a 5% variation should be tolerated to allow for manufacturing variance. We must demand dosing consistency in our drugs.

Let's just import what we need

This is a common attitude among the public and politicians. The American Association of Retired Persons endorses it and is organizing a grassroots campaign to support the idea. It saves all the work in trying to actually fix the problem—*or does it?*

It is common for retirees in Sun City, AZ, to carpool down to

[135] Banahan BF, Kolassa KM. *A physician survey on generic drugs and substitution of critical dose medications.* Archives of Internal Medicine. 1997 Oct 13;157(18):2080-8. http://www.ncbi.nlm.nih.gov/pubmed/9382664

[136] Approved Drug Products with Therapeutic Equivalence Evaluations, 29th Edition. U.S. Department of Health & Human Services, Food & Drug Administration, Center for Drug Evaluation and Research Office of Pharmaceutical science, Office of Generic Drugs; 2009, Page IX. http://www.fda.gov/ucm/groups/fdagov-public/@fdagov-drugs-gen/documents/document/ucm071436.pdf [Accessed 6/8/09].

Mexico for their medications every month or two to save money. In my hometown of Youngstown, OH, day-trips by bus are organized to take Americans to Canada for their prescription drugs. The Internet has a proliferation of advertisements and spam e-mails for cheap prescription drugs. Why should Americans have to pay top dollar? *(The answer is we shouldn't—but don't stop reading here.)*

While it might be all right to go to another First World country to purchase medication, it is not all right to run off to the Second or Third World to do so. Before anyone thinks this unfair, consider that one of the top issues each year at the World Health Organization's Annual Assembly is the problem of counterfeit products, whether fake, "watered" down or substituted, and the problem is increasing.

..Increasingly easy access to sophisticated technologies such as those for printing and manufacturing, have made it more difficult for governments and other concerned parties to combat counterfeiters of medical products effectively...the extent of counterfeiting is impossible to quantify...Counterfeiting affects all medical products: from medicines and pharmaceutical ingredients to medical devices and diagnostics...Counterfeit products have been detected in most of WHO's Member States and in all its regions. Cases have involved widely used medicines such as atorvastatin [Lipitor] and paracetamol [Tylenol], limited use medicines such as growth hormone, paclitaxal [Taxol], and filgrastim [Neupogen], erectile dysfunction medicines and medical devices such as contact lenses, condoms, surgical mesh and diagnostic test strips used by diabetic patients to monitor their blood glucose concentrations. Both expensive products and cheap ones, generic and branded products are being counterfeited with the result that they appear in community pharmacies and hospitals, as well as other less regulated settings.

Although organized crime and individuals acting alone have been associated with the manufacture and/or trade in, counterfeit medical products, in most cases the counterfeit products appear to have been internationally traded between previously unconnected groups or individuals. This fact puts an equal responsibility on importing and exporting countries.

Many factors of varying importance between Member states contribute to creating an environment where the manufacture of, and trade in, counterfeit medical products can thrive:
- Governments' unwillingness to recognize the existence or gravity of the problem
- Inadequate legal framework and penalties
- Weak administration and coordination, with measures not focused on fighting counterfeiting
- Ineffective control of manufacturing, import and distribution of medical products
- Ineffective collaboration among bodies and institutions, such as health authorities, police, customs and the judiciary, involved in regulation, control, investigation and prosecution
- Ineffective collaboration and exchange of information between the public and private sector
- Insufficient collaboration and exchange of information

Besides the ubiquitous corruption, several other socioeconomic factors, many of which are specific to some countries, or particular areas inside a country, undermine efforts against counterfeiting:
- National drug policies that prioritize economic over public health aspects of medicine manufacturing, with the result that exporting takes priority over compliance with good manufacturing practices.
- Extreme fragmentation of distribution channels involving an unnecessarily large number of transactions, thereby increasing the opportunities for counterfeiters to infiltrate the normal distribution system
- Existence of "extraterritorial" trade zones which largely escape from regulatory and enforcement oversight and goods and their accompanying documentation can be manipulated
- Inadequate access to health services and reliable pharmaceutical supply channels that creates opportunities for "informal operators" who establish "informal supply systems" purportedly to meet populations' real needs
- Absence of or insufficient social security coverage in countries that do not regulate prices; the resulting search by

patients for better prices often leads to fierce competition among vendors and opens opportunities for counterfeiters who can offer unbeatable prices

- Illiteracy and poverty, which puts patients at a particular disadvantage
- Unregulated Internet trade, where unscrupulous sellers can hide their identity and the true origin of traded medical products
- Third-party manufacturing, which, if not properly and carefully supervised, may lead to the unauthorized use of manufacturing techniques and packaging materials.[137]

Even legitimate importation of drugs by Big Pharma from their overseas manufacturing facilities has caused problems. Recall the heparin manufactured in China by Baxter Healthcare, which was contaminated by over-sulfonated chondroitin sulfate, a cheaper substance that somewhat mimics heparin's anticoagulant activity. This was deliberate sabotage by the chemists and managers working in the Chinese plant at the expense of the public.

The FDA's answer to counterfeit drugs and devices has been to open offices in Beijing, Guangzhou and Shanghai, other locations including India, the Middle East, Latin America and Europe. FDA employees are planning on inspecting products and developing liaisons with Chinese officials and groups. While developing liaisons with exporting governments is good, it is important to understand how ineffective it is for the FDA to go it alone on inspecting tours. According to a Reuter's article that ran in November 2007:

U.S. regulators inspect few foreign makers of pharmaceutical ingredients and have no accurate count of how many companies supply the American market, a watchdog arm of Congress said on Thursday. Data from the Food and Drug Administration suggest the agency inspects only 7 percent of foreign drugmakers each year, the Government Accountability Office (GAO) told lawmakers. The FDA lacks an accurate list of foreign sites subject to inspection because officials rely on conflicting databases, the GAO said. The agency cannot say how many of the overseas sites have never been visited, the GAO added.

Investigators uncovered similar problems when they reviewed the FDA's oversight of foreign drug manufacturers in 1998, said Marcia Crosse, the GAO's director of health-care issues. "Until FDA responds to systemic weaknesses in the management of this important program, it cannot provide the needed assurance that the drug supply reaching our citizens is appropriately scrutinized and safe," Crosse told the House of Representatives Energy and Commerce subcommittee on oversight and investigations.

Foreign-made medicines are common in Americans' medicine cabinets. More than 80 percent of active pharmaceutical ingredients now come from other countries, with more than half from India and China, lawmakers said.

The FDA is required to inspect U.S. drug plants every two years, but there is no set timeline for foreign facilities that supply drugs or their ingredients to the United States. One agency database lists more than 3,000 foreign sites registered to market drugs in the United States in fiscal 2007, while another put the number as high as 6,800. At the current pace, it would take the FDA 13 years to inspect each of the 3,000-plus firms once, the GAO said.

...William Hubbard, a former FDA associate commissioner, said the nation was vulnerable. "My concern is it's only a matter of time if we don't fix this," Hubbard said.

FDA Commissioner Andrew von Eschenbach said the agency was "taking an aggressive approach" to adapt to the rapid globalization of drug manufacturing. Initial steps include improving computer systems and deploying FDA personnel to foreign locations for long-term assignments. "We agree we must revamp our entire strategy ... we are doing this," von Eschenbach told the committee.

...Lawmakers will pursue legislation to give the FDA more funding for inspections and computer upgrades, said Michigan Democratic

Rep. Bart Stupak, the subcommittee chairman. "I believe we have an opportunity to fix FDA's foreign drug program before Americans are sickened or killed," he said.[138]

The bottom line is that the U.S. government does not have any money to waste. While we may set up offices in countries or cities where we have considerable business or there are an abundance of manufacturing facilities to facilitate trade, it is impractical to open offices everywhere. We do need to split up this task with our fellow First World countries that are also likely to be importing drugs from the same manufacturers.

Below is the text from a *Marketplace* Public Radio broadcast, by reporter Raymond Thibodeaux:

> **RAYMOND THIBODEAUX:** The FDA's inspectors have already raised safety concerns and banned at least four big Indian drug companies from exporting some of their products to the U.S, blocking about 30 products from Ranbaxy Pharmaceuticals, India's biggest pharma company. It prevented sales of Ranbaxy's generic versions of the antibiotic Cipro and the cholesterol pill Zocor.
>
> Ranbaxy declined an on-air interview, but in an e-mail response it said the FDA ban resulted from concerns about just two of its five plants in India.
>
> > **RANBAXY LETTER:** The FDA has said it has no evidence the drugs on the market are substandard and also that they comply with specifications upon testing. Ranbaxy will continue to co=operate with the FDA.

---

[138] Richwine, Lisa. *US inspects few foreign drugmakers, Congress told.* Reuters. November 1, 2007
http://www.reuters.com/article/marketsNews/idUKN0134236620071101?rpc=44&pageNumber=1&virtualBrandChannel=0

The company also says it will issue responses to FDA's concerns as appropriate. But some Indian business groups see the FDA's actions as outright "protectionism" brought about by the lobbying of big American drug companies at a time when the U.S. economy is at a downturn.

> **AJAY SAHAI:** Naturally, in that case you will try to find ways to restrict imports.

Ajay Sahai is executive director of the Federation of Indian Export Organizations.

> **SAHAI:** In many of the cases, Indian companies do have a case where they have been stopped by large companies present in the importing countries. They have tried to restrict the imports at whatever cost or citing whatever reason.

At the FDA's headquarters in Maryland, officials deny that accusation. Dr. Murray Lumpkin is the deputy commissioner of the FDA's Office of International Programs.

> **MURRAY LUMPKIN:** We really as a regulatory agency don't care where the products come from. It simply matters that they indeed are able to show us that they meet our standards for safety, quality and efficacy, and those standards are the same whether it's New Jersey or New Delhi.

India's government has vowed to take up the issue of protectionism with the U.S. But American public concern over tainted drug imports remains high and the FDA's overseas expansion will continue. The agency has plans for field offices in Latin America, the Middle East and Africa. It says this should speed up the approval process, get foreign drugs into U.S. stores sooner and bring down prices for American consumers.[139]

We cannot waste our government's resources putting offices in

---

[139] *FDA's overseas offices met with caution.* Raymond Thibodeaux Interview for Marketplace, Public Radio; April 27, 2009. © 2009 American Public Media. Used with permission. All rights reserved.
http://marketplace.publicradio.org/display/web/2009/04/27/pm_fda_crackdown/

every country that might wish to export drugs to us. If foreign facilities have not been inspected and products randomly tested by us or our First World trading partners, then their products should be quarantined on entry until random samples from each shipment are tested either by the FDA or a government-authorized independent laboratory, at the expense of the exporter.

When pharmaceutical companies want to import medicines from their overseas facilities other than ones in another First World country, those facilities should be required to employ First World expats as the general managers, senior staff and QA personnel. This is not being elitist. The major problem in the Third World is the state of mind, rather than a lack of money; what is and is not acceptable there is often considerably different than in the First World. Consider Europe after the Second World War. Despite the devastation in a city like Milan, a good deal of the destruction had been repaired within seven years and commerce was functioning normally. Yet seven years after going into Iraq and hundreds of billions of dollars later, we have yet to see what resembles a First World country. We won both wars, but the success of the people in creating or recreating a First World country is vastly different. Italy was already a First World country. In the First World, people have a different set of standards and expectations for themselves and how they do business, including how they provide goods and services. In the Third World, particularly in the former communist countries I have worked in, the mentality tends to resemble a form of Ferengi capitalism.[140] A Third World country

---

[140] For non-Trekkies: The Ferengi are alien creatures in the Star Trek Deep Space Nine series; their behavior is governed by the 286 Rules of Acquisition. They are greedy and generally

generally does not move to a First World country in one generation. It usually takes two generations of education and seeing First World business practices for a country to move up into the First World.[141] Until then, expat management is essential.

While we should be clear about the process and pleasant to those exporters who wish to comply, we should not let any country twist our arm by bringing politics into the situation. We should not tolerate the importation of drugs from overseas manufacturers with lower manufacturing standards than our own. This is a quality and safety issue. The FDA has a responsibility first and foremost to protect the American people.

Food as a drug—You are what you eat

As a board-certified physician in both occupational medicine and public health & general preventive medicine, I would be remiss if I did not explore the role of the FDA in food safety.

Food has been regulated by the FDA since the early part of the 20th century. However, in our great search for wisdom and knowledge, it appears we sometimes lose good judgment and common sense. President Obama says we should seek to find a cure for cancer in our time. This is a noble and worthy goal. As an agency of the Department of Health and Human Services, one might think that the FDA would do everything within the confines of its mandate to assist

---

less than scrupulous; their only interest is profit at any and all costs. For examples see http://memory-alpha.org/en/wiki/Ferengi_Rules_of_Acquisition

[141] South Korea is a prime example of this; it is a lovely 1st world country today, as witnessed by the world during the 1988 Seoul Winter Olympics.

in that process.

One key area the FDA regulates is food additives.

What is a Food Additive?
"Food additive" is defined by the Food and Drug Administration (FDA) as any substance used to provide a technical effect in foods. The use of food additives has become more prominent in recent years, due to the increased production of prepared, processed, and convenience foods. Additives are used for flavor and appeal, food preparation and processing, freshness, and safety...

Who Monitors the Safety of Food Additives?
Before any substance can be added to food, its safety must be assessed in a stringent approval process. The Food Safety and Inspection Service (FSIS) of the U.S. Department of Agriculture (USDA) shares responsibility with FDA for the safety of food additives used in meat, poultry, and egg products. All additives are initially evaluated for safety by FDA.

When an additive is proposed for use in a meat, poultry, or egg product, its safety, technical function, and conditions of use must also be evaluated by the Labeling and Consumer Protection Staff of FSIS, as provided in the Federal Meat Inspection Act, the Poultry Products Inspection Act, the Egg Products Inspection Act, and related regulations. Although FDA has overriding authority regarding additive safety, FSIS may apply even stricter standards that take into account the unique characteristics of meat, poultry, and egg products. Several years ago, for instance, permission was sought to use sorbic acid in meat salads. Although sorbic acid was an approved food additive, permission for use in meat salad was denied because such usage could mask spoilage caused by organisms that cause foodborne illness.

Additives are never given permanent approval. FDA and FSIS continually review the safety of approved additives, based on the best scientific knowledge, to determine if approvals should be modified or withdrawn...

When Did Food Additives Regulations Begin?
The 1958 Food Additives Amendment to the Federal Food, Drug, and Cosmetic Act provided for the first specific regulations of food additives. Approval of new food additives was required before they could be marketed, and *the responsibility for proving their safety was placed on the manufacturer*...If it is approved as safe under the proposed conditions of use, FDA prescribes in its regulations, the types of foods it may be used in, and how it may be used.

Are Any Additives Exempt from the Approval Process?
The Food Additives Amendment exempted two groups of food additives from FDA's testing and approval process. One is the list of substances known as "generally recognized as safe" (GRAS). This group includes a variety of substances, from commonly used flavorings and spices to phosphates and carrageenan. These substances are considered harmless under prescribed conditions of use. Past extensive use of these substances has produced no known harmful effects. The other group of additives known as "substances with prior sanction" was approved by USDA and FDA for use in foods prior to the passage of the 1958 Food Additives Amendment. Examples of these types of substances include potassium nitrite and sodium nitrite. Additives can be removed from the lists if tests indicate the substances are not safe for human consumption.[142]

According to the USDA website, it is the duty of the FSIS and particularly the FDA to continually evaluate additives based on available science. Unfortunately, that is not necessarily happening. Sometimes, it seems that their scientific objectivity has been compromised by attempts to justify previous approvals, possibly at the health expense of the American people.

"A little more carcinogen with my pancakes please."

---

[142] US Department of Agriculture Web site
http://www.fsis.usda.gov/Fact_Sheets/Additives_in_Meat_&_Poultry_Products/index.asp
[Accessed 6/8/09]

Let us look at the common additive sodium benzoate. This is a preservative that is in everything from soft drinks to pancake syrup to lemon juice. It is used as a preservative in toothpastes, cosmetics and mouthwashes. It is chiefly an antimicrobial agent. In fairness, some sodium benzoate occurs naturally in foods such as cranberries and apples, but it does not seem to act as a preservative for them, which may suggest that it is bound differently in nature.

The New Zealand food safety authorities note that "Benzene can be formed at very low levels in beverages that contain both ascorbic acid (vitamin C) and sodium benzoate."[143]

Critics will say that just a little bit of benzene is produced—it is measured in parts per million and billion. The FDA has been aware of this problem since 1990. "C. Glen Lawrence, now a biochemist and professor at Long Island University, performed the FDA tests that documented the problem in the early 1990s when he worked for the agency as a science advisor. 'People at FDA who were testing foods told me they found benzene in orange soda,' Lawrence said. 'I said, "I think it must be coming from the sodium benzoate."' Lawrence said he was able to demonstrate that sodium benzoate and ascorbic acid in soft drinks reacted to form benzene. He published his findings in the Journal of Agricultural and Food Chemistry in 1993."[144]

The FDA Consumer Magazine noted that:

---

[143] New Zealand Food Safety Authority Web site
http://www.nzfsa.govt.nz/consumers/chemicals-nutrients-additives-and-toxins/benzene-in-drinks/index.htm [Accessed 6/8/09]
[144] Havala Hobbs, S. *FDA Knew of Benzene Problem in Sodas Years Ago*. Charlotte Observer, March 8, 2006.

...The FDA has no regulatory limits for benzene in beverages other than bottled water. The U.S. Environmental Protection Agency has established a maximum contaminant level for benzene of 5 parts per billion (ppb) in drinking water. The FDA has adopted this level for bottled water as a quality standard...

From the start of the survey in November through April 2006, the FDA tested more than 100 soft drinks and other beverages. Beverage samples were collected from retail stores in Maryland, Virginia, and Michigan. The survey is not a reflection of the distribution of benzene in beverages in the U.S. food supply. The data cover a limited number of products and brands, and limited geographic areas. Even though the data are limited, Kidwell says, the FDA believes that the results indicate that benzene levels are not a safety concern for consumers...

The CFSAN found benzene levels above 5 ppb in five of the beverage products tested: Crystal Light Sunrise Classic Orange, Crush Pineapple, Safeway Select Diet Orange Soda, AquaCal Strawberry Flavored Water Beverage, and Giant Light Cranberry Juice Cocktail...The FDA has contacted those firms whose products were found to contain more than 5 ppb benzene in the CFSAN survey. Manufacturers have reformulated the products to reduce or eliminate benzene, and some have sent samples to the CFSAN for analysis. Thus far, the CFSAN has tested *a few* of the reformulated products provided by the manufacturers and found that benzene levels were less than 1 ppb...[145]

While the FDA knew there was a problem, they did not ban the chemical from being put in soft drinks. They did not conduct nationwide testing and only retested a few of the supposedly reformulated products. Yet the problem appears to have been whitewashed. Is this good science?

No doubt their excuse will be that "the dose makes the poison," and there was only a small amount in some of the soft drinks tested.

---

[145] Meadows, Michelle. *Benzene in Beverages.* FDA Consumer Magazine. 2006 Sep-Oct;40(5):9-10.

But this is not the only place we are exposed to this chemical. The cumulative daily load of sodium benzoate and potassium benzoate, and therefore benzene, which an individual receives also depends on the products used and the dietary habits of a person. Even if the chemical is "safe" in an individual food, it may be unsafe when eaten in combination with other foods. Consider the parent who pours his child a glass of orange juice while making pancakes for breakfast. The pancake syrup contains sodium benzoate. Unknowingly, this loving parent has just created a poisonous combination. (In addition, studies have linked this preservative with hyperactivity.) Start reading labels and you will find that sodium or potassium benzoate is ubiquitous in our food supply. Think of that co-worker you see washing down their vitamins with a big gulp diet soda.

While sodium or potassium benzoate is still in soft drinks, such as Diet Coke, Diet Pepsi, Diet 7-Up, Crush, Dr. Pepper and Mountain Dew in this country, the U.K. newspaper the *Daily Mail* reported last year that "Soft drink giant Coca-Cola is phasing out a controversial additive that has been linked to hyperactivity and causing damage to DNA. The chemical Sodium Benzoate, also known as E211, is used to stop fizzy drinks (from) going moldy…Peter Piper, a professor of molecular biology research at Sheffield University found that the additive could switch off vital parts of DNA that could be linked to cirrhosis of the liver and Parkinson's disease."[146]

---

[146] Fenandez, Colin. *Coca-cola to phase out controversial chemical linked to hyperactivity and gene damage*. The Daily Mail. May 25, 2008. http://www.dailymail.co.uk/news/article-1021809/Coca-cola-phase-controversial-chemical-linked-hyperactivity-gene-damage.html

...Like Professor Piper, Professor Vyvyan Howard, professor of bio-imaging at the University of Ulster, questions the practice of approving additives for use that have been tested alone. But in 2005, Professor Howard led a Liverpool University study that showed that, when combined, some additives in crisps and fizzy drinks had seven times the effect they had singly...

Another study, conducted by the University of Southampton in 2004, had even more alarming findings for parents. Researchers gave 277 3- and 4-year-olds on the Isle of Wight either a placebo drink or a drink containing additives. Their parents, who did not know what their child had been given, were asked to rate their child's hyperactivity. The number of children showing extreme hyperactivity on the additive-free diet was more than halved, falling from 15 to 6 per cent.

...According to Professor Piper, sodium benzoate has a destructive effect on living cells, destroying the DNA in the mitochondria. In essence, his laboratory tests on yeast cells suggest that such preservatives generate free radicals which, in turn, damage cells. This oxidative damage, he says, is the kind done by ageing and by alcoholic binges. Professor Piper is disappointed at what he sees as a "complacency" among the soft-drinks industry over the potential dangers of additives.

He believes the industry has been relying on safety tests that are old and incomplete and has chosen to prioritize other research in other areas. "If they do any basic research, it's more into whether it tastes good rather than trying to reduce additives and make it more natural."

He stressed that he was not saying that sodium benzoate was unsafe, but that the food industry could not state with certainty that it was safe. "We are feeding vast amounts of them to children inadvertently. Is this a completely safe process? This is what we have to worry about."

...Nonetheless, manufacturers and retailers have begun to remove additives from food and drinks. Sainsbury's will have removed almost all artificial colorings, flavorings and benzoate preservatives by the end of June. Marks & Spencer will phase out additives by the end of this year. And Asda will do the same for its own-brand products by the end of 2007.[147]

Clearly, this additive can be eliminated from our food supply. This is already being done elsewhere. Why is the FDA allowing carcinogens to be voluntarily put in our food, cosmetics and oral hygiene products?

A document released by the International Program on Chemical Safety, a joint program between the International Labor Organization, the World Health Organization and the UN Environmental Program, had this to say regarding benzoates:

> There are a few analyses of processed foodstuffs available... Generally, the actual uptake depends on the individual's choice of food to be consumed and the different limit values in different countries. Several intake estimations have been published...
>
> A frequent contributor to dietary exposure is soft drinks. A rough estimation based on the average daily consumption in Germany of such drinks (372 ml non-alcoholic beverages...; BAGS, 1995) by 19- to 24-year-old men, assuming the concentration of benzoic acid present corresponds to a maximum allowable level of 150 mg/liter (EC, 1995), would result in a mean daily intake of 55.8 mg benzoic acid per person (or 0.80 mg/kg body weight, assuming a 70-kg body weight). For comparison, a similar calculation with sugar-free marmalade, jam, and similar spreads, which are allowed to contain higher levels of benzoic acid (500 mg/kg; EC, 1995), would result in a possible intake of 4.1 mg per person per day, or 0.06 mg/kg body weight per day (assumes a daily consumption of 8.2 g, according to BAGS, 1995). *This was more than a possible intake via fruits containing natural benzoic acid...*
>
> The Joint FAO/WHO Expert Committee on Food Additives (JECFA) assessed the intake of benzoates from information

---

[147] *E211 Revealed: Evidence highlights new fear over drinks additive* The Independent. May 27, 2007. http://www.independent.co.uk/life-style/health-and-families/health-news/e211-revealed-evidence-highlights-new-fear-over-drinks-additive-450594.html

provided by nine countries (Australia, China, Finland, France, Japan, New Zealand, Spain, United Kingdom, and USA) (WHO, 1999). Because diets differ among countries, the foods that contribute to benzoate intake would be expected to vary. The food category that contributed most to benzoate intake was soft drinks (carbonated, water-based, flavored drinks) for Australia/New Zealand, France, the United Kingdom, and the USA…Soy sauce was the main source of benzoate in China and the second most important in Japan. *The best estimates of national mean intakes of benzoates by consumers ranged from 0.18 mg/kg body weight per day in Japan to 2.3 mg/kg body weight per day in the USA.* These estimates were based on analyses involving either model diets or individual dietary records and maximum limits specified by national governments or the European Union…

Quantitative information on (oral or dermal/mucosal) exposure via cosmetic, hygienic, or medical products is rare, but the data available indicate a remarkable contribution to exposure. There are reports on leaching of benzoic acid from denture-base acrylic resins. After 10 days of immersion in artificial saliva, concentrations of up to about 3 mg/liter have been observed for benzoic acid, which is formed as a degradation product of the benzoyl peroxide that is added as a polymerization initiator (Koda et al., 1989, 1990)…Use of the toothpaste with the highest concentration (by 40 20-year-old female students) would result in a calculated daily intake of about 2.23 mg per person. This was about the same amount as their estimated intake from diet (Ishida, 1996)… [148]

The estimated consumption of benzoates in the United States was the highest in the nine country study. How much sodium benzoate is converted into benzene depends on individual habits and preferences. Benzene is a known carcinogen. "The seriousness of poisoning caused by benzene depends on the amount, route, and length of time of exposure, as well as the age and pre-existing medical condition of

---

[148]Wibbertmann A., Keilhorn J, Koennecker G., Mangelsdorf I., Melber,C. *International Program on Chemical Safety: Concise International Chemical Assessment Document No. 26: Benzoic Acid and Sodium Benzoate* http://www.inchem.org/documents/cicads/cicads/cicad26.htm [Last accessed 6/8/09]

the exposed person."[149] It is known to cause aplastic anemia, acute myelogenous leukemia, non-Hodgkin's lymphoma, multiple myeloma, and neurotoxicity. A multitude of studies have demonstrated it to be harmful over the last 80 years.[150] It is a chemical whose exposure we monitor in the industrial setting. Why is it alright to put anything that might be converted to it in our food? No additional studies need to be done. It is a bad idea; it should be stopped.

Just a little arsenic every day won't hurt me will it?

Let us look at another chemical that has made the news recently, Bisphenol A. This product is used to line our food and beverage cans. It is also used to make polycarbonate plastics. You will find it in any plastic with a number 7 on the recycling icon. It has been used in everything from plastic baby bottles, sippy cups and medical plastics. Over 90% of Americans have detectable levels of this substance in their bodies. It has estrogen-like activity and has been linked to cardiovascular disease, diabetes, thyroid dysfunction, low sperm counts, prostate cancer and breast cancer. Use of this chemical has increased in recent years. It can leech out into the substances in the container.

According to the FDA's *Draft Assessment of Bisphenol A for use in Food Contact Applications*:

---

[149] CDC Web site http://www.bt.cdc.gov/agent/benzene/basics/facts.asp [Accessed 6/8/09]
[150] Agency for Toxic Substances and Disease Registry Toxicity Profile for Benzene http://www.atsdr.cdc.gov/toxprofiles/tp3-c3.pdf [Accessed 6/20/09]

In estimating adult exposure, FDA analyzed BPA levels in select canned vegetables purchased in Washington, D.C. metro supermarkets and packed in imported and domestic manufactured cans containing epoxy-based coating enamels. *The test samples consisted of canned mushrooms (3 samples), tomatoes, artichokes, and mixed vegetables (1 sample each) and included both the pureed vegetable and liquid.* The test samples were analyzed for BPA by HPLC with fluorescence detection, with an LOD of 5 ppb. BPA levels ranged from 5-39 ppb in vegetables, with an average value of 16 ppb for all **6 *samples***. FDA also considered a study by Brotons *et al.* in which BPA levels were analyzed in select canned vegetables purchased in U.S. or Spanish supermarkets. *Test samples consisted of the liquid phases of canned peas, artichokes, green beans, mixed vegetables, corn, mushrooms, asparagus, palm hearts, peppers, and tomatoes.* The test samples were analyzed for BPA by HPLC and ranged from 12-76 ppb (four samples were non-detect), *with an average value of 22 ppb for all **10 samples***. FDA considers that an individual's diet typically consists of a variety of canned vegetables; therefore, an average level of 22 ppb BPA in vegetables is sufficiently conservative for estimating exposure to BPA from epoxy-based can enamels. **FDA *assumed* that the levels are representative of all food (i.e., aqueous, acidic, alcoholic, and fatty) packed in coated cans.** This is known as the "weight-averaged" concentration of BPA in food (i.e., [the] average is 22 ppb. FDA has determined that **17% of all food available to consumers for purchase is packaged in polymer coated metal packaging** and; therefore, the appropriate consumption factor (CF) for calculating exposure is 0.17. Using FDA's traditional approach of combining migration values and CF, the corresponding average dietary concentration of BPA from can enamels has been calculated by multiplying 22 ppb by 0.17 (22 ppb x 0.17) resulting in a dietary concentration of 3.7 ppb (equivalent to an intake of 0.185 µg/kg bw/day for a 60 kg person consuming 3 kg of food per day.[151]

As you can see, the total sample size was 16. That is correct—after testing all of 16 cans, the FDA determined that 17% of our entire food supply was safe. It would seem any high school chemistry class could

---

[151] *Draft Assessment for BisPhenol A use for Food Contact Applications.* Food & Drug Administration, Draft version August 14, 2008. Food & Drug Administration Web site http://www.fda.gov/ohrms/dockets/ac/08/briefing/2008-0038b1_01_02_FDA%20BPA%20Draft%20Assessment.pdf [Accessed 6/21/09]

have designed a better study and surely would have thought to test more than 16 cans! For some reason the FDA thought it was essential to test three cans of mushrooms—who knew mushrooms were such a popular vegetable? Perhaps they were different brands?

> ...a marked discordance exists between the currently accepted ADI [acceptable daily intake dose] for BPA of 50 µg/kg per day and numerous adverse effects in animals occurring at levels far below this dosage in recent experiments using the tools of 21st-century biology. A fundamental problem is that the current ADI for BPA is based on experiments conducted in the early 1980s using outdated methods (only very high doses were tested) and insensitive assays. *More recent findings from independent scientists were rejected by the FDA, apparently because those investigators did not follow the outdated testing guidelines for environmental chemicals, whereas studies using the outdated, insensitive assays (predominantly involving studies funded by the chemical industry) are given more weight* in arriving at the conclusion that BPA is not harmful at current exposure levels...Second, along with the exponential increase in the use of BPA in products during the last 30 years, there has been a dramatic increase in the incidence of obesity and type 2 diabetes in children. Very low doses of BPA during fetal/neonatal life in rodents increase the rate of postnatal growth as well as advance puberty, with subsequent disruption of neuroendocrine function.[152]

Yet "chemical manufacturers continue to discount these published findings because no industry-funded studies have reported significant effects of low doses of BPA, although greater than 90% of government-funded studies have reported significant effects."[153] The

---

[152] vom Saal FS, Myers JP. *Bisphenol A and Risk of Metabolic Disorders*. JAMA, September 17, 2008; 300: 1353 – 1355. http://jama.ama-assn.org/cgi/reprint/300/11/1353?maxtoshow=&HITS=10&hits=10&RESULTFORMAT=&fulltext=%22bisphenol+a%22&searchid=1&FIRSTINDEX=0&resourcetype=HWCIT

[153] vom Saal FS, Hughes C. *An Extensive New Literature Concerning Low-Dose Effects of Bisphenol A Shows the Need for a New Risk Assessment*. Environmental Health Perspectives. 2005 August; 113(8): 926–933. http://www.pubmedcentral.nih.gov/articlerender.fcgi?artid=1280330 This is an Open Access article: verbatim copying and redistribution of this article are permitted in all media for any

latest research shows that this chemical is not rapidly metabolized and excreted, as long thought. Instead, it may accumulate in the fatty tissue of the body.[154] You do not have to understand all of the gritty science to know that this chemical is a public health hazard. The question is, why does the FDA allow it in our food, when we have known for years in occupational medicine that this chemical is harmful?

[154] Stahlhut RW, Welshons WV, Swan SH. *Bisphenol A Data in NHANES Suggest Longer than Expected Half-Life, Substantial Nonfood Exposure, or Both.* Environmental Health Perspectives, May 2009; 115 (5): 784-789.
http://www.ehponline.org/members/2009/0800376/0800376.pdf

Chapter 11

Those big, bad insurers

Insurers are another group we love to hate. Physicians and patients tend to see them as obstructionists. Historically, under the indemnity plans in the 1960s and 1970s, insurers paid all expenses. When managed care took a serious foothold, particularly with HMO plans, it seemed the practice was to deny every request and see if the doctor and/or patient protested. Nowadays, that is not generally the objective of utilization review teams at insurance companies. In fact, if that were found to be the case today, they would be subject to class action "bad faith" claims by their insureds. Additionally, they would be the subject of state insurance commission investigations.

Unfortunately, neither physicians nor patients are taught how to effectively work with insurers to get things done expediently and decrease the likelihood of non-certification of requests for services and treatments.

What's in a policy?

Working in the insurance industry, I have learned that insurers will write a quote for any type of policy that employers are willing to buy. What is amazing to me is how many variations of coverage versus a standard plan employers will request. In fact, so much so, that I have questioned the sales teams more than once, who said, "We tried to tell them, but this is what they wanted." A CEO may want the genetic test for BRCA included in coverage for employees, because his family has a history of breast cancer and he believes this is an important test. Then there are the politically correct healthcare plans. These come from employers who insist that erectile dysfunction drugs for their male employees should be covered under the plan, because women have their birth control covered. Think through the logic of that proposal. Presumably women are using birth control to limit pregnancies and children, which add to both the medical costs and the number of plan members. On the other hand, men are using this drug for recreational purposes. Political correctness aside—with limited resources, what makes financial sense for the employer with limited resources? Frankly, all these variations make administering a plan more challenging. Additionally, they don't provide the most coverage for the money.

There is no such thing as a good or bad health plan. *Employees get the plans for which their employer paid.* If employees want a particular benefit, they should let their human resources department know. Most good employers will at least look into modifying the policy. Good employers are responsive and want to keep their employees happy, provided it is not cost-prohibitive.

Good stewards or stingy Scrooges!

Let us follow where the money actually goes. The important
numbers to look at are the medical-cost ratios. This is the actual
amount of premium collected that is spent on medical expenses. This
does not include administrative costs. Look at what these numbers
have been recently:

> Aetna's higher-than-expected medical-cost ratio -- 83% of every
> premium dollar spent on care -- managed to overshadow a rise in
> profit for the quarter, sending its stock downward after earnings
> were released.[155]

> A new report released by the California Medical Assn. reveals that
> during the last fiscal year… ending June 30, 2007…Great-West
> Healthcare of California had the lowest medical-loss ratio, at 69.4%.
> Great-West was recently bought by Cigna, which had one of the
> highest medical-loss ratios at 94.3%. WellPoint-owned Blue Cross
> of California (now known as Anthem Blue Cross) had the second-
> lowest medical-loss ratio at 79%, and Blue Shield was fifth lowest,
> at 82.1%. Kaiser Foundation Health Plan had a ratio of 90.6%. L.A.
> Care Health Plan, a public health plan with fewer than 1 million
> members had the highest of any plan, with 97.1% of revenue going
> to care…

> Twenty-four other states mandate medical-loss ratios, although only
> five do so across both group and individual markets…The current

---

[155] Berry, E. *Analysts focus on health plans' medical cost numbers*. American Medical News.
Posted May 18, 2009.
 http://www.ama-assn.org/amednews/2009/05/18/bisb0518.htm

highest is 82% minimum medical-loss ratio required in Minnesota for some insurers offering small group policies.[156]

So what's the problem with 97% of money going out the door to pay for care? There is no money to pay the cost of administering the claims!

What are typical administrative costs? It depends on the plan, but the typical costs have remained about the same for the last several years. "In 2000, the administrative cost ratio was 11 percent for Blue Cross and Blue Shield Plans, versus 11.6 percent for the industry as a whole."[157] You might think the bigger the plan, the greater the economies of scale in administration, but Andrew Naugle at the actuarial consulting firm, Milliman, says:

> Our research on this topic, however, suggests that economies of scale aren't as significant as one might intuitively think when it comes to administrative costs. On the contrary, we find that the most significant administrative cost reductions due to scale economies occur as organizations grow from zero to approximately 500,000 members. Significant marginal savings are achieved across all functional areas as organizations grow from zero to 100,000 members. Between 100,000 and 500,000 members, the marginal savings are less and tend to be centralized among a few functional areas. Beyond a plan size of 500,000 members, the marginal savings are limited to specific functional areas and quickly diminish to a point where they become more difficult to quantify. This is not to

---

[156] Berry E. *Report details how much insurers spend on care in California.* American Medical News, July 21, 2008.
http://www.ama-assn.org/amednews/2008/07/21/bisc0721.htm
[157] Sacia, KJ, Dobson RH. *Health Plan Administrative Cost Trends*. Milliman, February 20, 2003. BCBS Web site http://www.bcbs.com/blueresources/cost/admin-cost-trends.html?templateName=template-28719196&print=t and *Understanding Health Plan Administrative Costs*, Blue Cross Blue Shield Association Web site http://www.bcbs.com/blueresources/cost/Cost_Admin030703.pdf

say there aren't other advantages to having a high number of members, including the clout that comes with such scale.[158]

A rule of thumb is that about 85% goes out the door to pay claims. Around 10% goes to administration. My old employer, Highmark, is a nonprofit insurer and explicitly states that it tries to keep the med-loss ratio at 90%.[159] It may vary slightly in any given year. Nonprofits are given this tax status because they provide a needed service to the public. The nonprofit carriers are good for the industry as they keep the for-profit insurers honest in a competitive marketplace. The for-profits have incentive to reduce administrative costs and are constrained from overcharging customers. Likewise the for-profit carriers force the not-for-profits to keep administrative costs within reason.

What goes into pricing premiums? There are three main factors that determine premiums. The first involves the experience rating for the employer group or individual. If you have had an auto accident, the company's experience with you has not been good. As a result, your auto insurance premiums will go up. Health insurance is a bit more complex. Insurers take actuarial data and try to predict the future claims given the age of the individual or the average age of the employer group, past claims data, diagnoses, etc. Secondly, insurers try to predict the rate of increase in medical costs for the coming year. And finally, an area rarely, if ever, discussed is role of interest rates. Insurers need to be solvent. Depending on tax status and state

---

[158] Naugle, A. *Optimizing Administrative Expenses*. Milliman Web site [Accessed 6/20/09] http://www.milliman.com/perspective/healthreform/optimizing-admin-expenses-HCR01-31-08.php

[159] Stouffer, R. *Highmark's profits fell 75 percent during 2008*. Pittsburgh Tribune Review, April 2, 2009. http://pittsburghlive.com/x/pittsburghtrib/business/s_618919.html

regulations, insurers may be required to invest a certain percentage of premiums collected "conservatively" in treasuries, government-backed securities, government agencies or grade "A" commercial paper. In fact, nonprofits may be required to keep over 90% of their reserves in such investments. Nonprofit insurers will use any investment gains to offset costs and rises in premium, which helps keep rates lower for consumers. Because for-profits must have competitive rates, they may also use a portion of their investment proceeds similarly. With the Federal Reserve Bank keeping interest rates artificially low the past few years, and now essentially zero, there is no additional revenue to offset rate increases for customers which has forced premiums upward.

It has been reported that health plan administrative requirements cost the average doctor and his office personnel $68,274 per physician per year.[160] It also costs insurers considerable time and money. With the type of medical records system proposed in Chapter 5, tens of billions of dollars could be saved.[161] It would greatly decrease the utilization review and precertification processes. It could save money in a number of other ways, too. For example, upon approval, a list of several of the low-cost providers of diagnostic services might be generated for the patient and emailed or mailed as a convenience and cost-containment measure. As we saw in Chapter 4, there is no need to pay $1,519 for a chest x-ray when $120 will get you the same information.

---

[160] Berry E. *Health plan requirements cost practices billions*. American Medical News. June 1, 2009. http://www.ama-assn.org/amednews/2009/06/01/bil20601.htm
[161] Ibid.

An electronic medical record would also facilitate the claims processing and payment side. No longer will providers and insurers have to go through this dance: The insurer sends a fax requesting copies of the records. The provider bills the insurer for retrieval. The insurer cuts a check for the records. The provider sends them (or not) to the insurer. Claims processors review them for accuracy and payment. This is incredibly time-intensive and slows down processing considerably. With the secure, authenticated EMR system proposed, the provider would simply submit the claim for payment, and the payor could instantly verify what was or was not done for the patient. It would be much more difficult for fraud and abuse to occur if insurers had access to the total record, as opposed to just the pages the provider wanted the insurer to see.

Disease management

Companies are increasingly asking about disease management programs offered by their insurers. They have heard about the potential of these programs to keep their employees healthier and save their health plans money. They work very well for the management of certain diseases, such as diabetes, asthma or congestive heart failure. There are currently Phase II clinical trials looking at the effectiveness of high- and low-intensity disease management for smoking cessation at the University of Kansas. It will be interesting to see what the evidence proves. When considering these programs, let the buyer beware; the content and quality varies considerably. Employers should make certain the savings figures presented represent the total cost of the program *with* administrative costs. They must also verify the program is equivalent to the one used in the study, or the return on investment may not be replicated.

The biggest obstacle to overcome is getting employees to participate in the program. It helps if employers let their employees know that they have purchased the service, so employees are not surprised if they receive a letter in the mail or a call from the disease management nurse. Without forewarning, employees can get quite hostile, feeling that their privacy has somehow been violated or that their employer has people "spying" on them. This is not the case; medical information remains confidential. Their employer is only trying to get them to better understand their disease and manage it. All data collected is aggregated for reporting results and cost-benefit analysis. The employer can help increase participation if they offer incentives to their employees. (See Chapter 9 - Becoming better companies.)

Making utilization review work

One of the least understood areas for doctors and patients is the utilization review process. This is when your plan language requires that the doctor or pharmacy call in to pre-certify a certain test, procedure or medication. Yes, this is done to contain costs, but it is a serious misunderstanding to believe that is the only purpose.

Often drugs, tests and procedures become popular with physicians because they heard about them at their latest continuing medical education meeting or read a study in a journal. Doctors are no more immune to advertising or good publicity than the rest of the population. Everyone wants to be on the proverbial cutting edge and give their patients the best care. However, these new drugs and tests can be very costly, and, like coronary CT angiography with calcium scoring, may not necessarily mean anything. Unless it is a landmark study, with many participants and good study design, a single study does not change the *standard of care*. How many times have we heard one study show something promising to be the next "magic bullet" cure, only to be to be contradicted a few months later as useless? Medicine requires a "body of evidence" to support such changes in practice. Until we have that, it is still investigational or experimental. The major insurers have written policy papers on various high-ticket drugs, tests and procedures. These are well-documented with the appropriate scientific literature and reviewed for changes or updates regularly.

This past year my company received a request for a certain chemotherapy regimen to treat a cancer. The nurse came to me to verify the treatment, as she did not see it in the National Comprehensive Cancer Network (NCCN) protocols – neither did I. We called the provider and asked him to send us evidence for his request, because it did not appear to follow protocols. He said, "I am on the NCCN Review Committee for this disease. About a month ago, a landmark study, with over 1,200 people came out showing this treatment regimen was far superior to anything else. I have been talking with my colleagues on the committee; this protocol is on the agenda to be updated at our next meeting." He sent a copy of the study; we verified what he said with NCCN and certified the treatment.

First and foremost, if you want to get a procedure or test certified, e-mail, fax or send in the information to your carrier that demonstrates the patient meets the criteria for the request and the appropriate workup was done. If you want cutting edge, then be prepared to show the scientific evidence supporting your rationale. This is how to get things done.

Self-insured versus Fully-insured companies

Stop-loss or excess-risk is a "reinsurance" product for employer groups who are self-insured, with regard to health insurance. These are companies that are big enough to bear the risk and pay for their own healthcare. It allows them to save money on "unused" premiums they would have paid out if they were fully insured, but protects against a catastrophic claim.

Usually, these are large employer groups with over 100 employees. In a given year, when an employee or covered member of the employee's family reaches a certain dollar amount in claims (also known as the "attachment point" or "specific deductible")[162] notification of the claim is sent by the employer's TPA to the stop-loss carrier. The carrier then picks up the tab for each additional dollar of expenses that year. If there is a known catastrophic case, underwriters may place a higher attachment point on an individual member of the

---

[162] This is equivalent to a deductible for that company for that person. It may be set in the tens or hundreds of thousands of dollars. Some companies set an aggregate deductible that limits the total amount for which the entire company would be responsible.

group. While this increases the possible amount an employer may be responsible for one employee, it allows the carrier to offer a lower quotation for the group, at a more fair and competitive price. This is so one outlier does not skew the rating of an otherwise fairly healthy employee population. While there are carriers who will not "laser" a cat claim, as it is called in the industry, the result is always higher rates for the group.

It amazes me that there are still employers who incorporate limited or no utilization review or case management in the third party administration of their self-insured policies. I believe they are misguided in thinking they are providing a "no hassle" policy for their employees while saving a few dollars. They are only looking at the discounts the TPA can give them, but they are missing the opportunity to limit overutilization. However, when a large claim comes in (particularly an out-of-network claim) and the TPA notifies them of the need to write a check, they get quite upset. "How did this happen?" is a familiar question. It is simple. No notification was required. Without notification, the TPA cannot go to the out-of-network provider to negotiate a discount, nor can they alert the employee to use an in-network provider or face increased out-of-pocket costs. In fairness, TPAs are very good at paying claims. They may get additional discounts from the facilities for prompt payment that may be greater than the amounts they earn from administering the claim. These may or may not be passed on to the employer group. They tend to pay little scrutiny to the actual charges; there is almost never line-by-line auditing of cat claims. They start paying closer attention to the bills when they get close to a specific deductible, because the reinsurer will start raising questions if there is a problem.

Employers who are large enough to self-insure may flip back to a fully insured product depending on employee mix, as well as the market for insurance, which hardens and softens in cycles approximately every four to six years.

Smaller companies generally have no choice but to fully insure themselves. It is hard on small employer groups with less than 50, and particularly less than 25, employees. One employee with a shock claim really skews the rates for these groups. It makes it hard for these groups to offer insurance to their employees because underwriters will say the group's "experience rating" has changed. Experience ratings base premiums on the amount of claims in the prior year. It is the same mechanism that increases your car insurance rates increase after an accident. This is why someone who has had a previous cat claim will likely not get a private individual policy, without an exclusion for that condition or a high deductible, if at all.

A word about other types of carriers

Insurers that are perhaps the most incentivized to help the doctor help the patient get back to a normal life are the workers' compensation (WC) and disability insurers. They can help get the tools the patient needs to resume a degree of normalcy. They can assist in getting ergonomic evaluations of the workplace, voice-activated software, seeing eye dogs, job retraining, motorized wheel chairs, etc. While WC provides medical benefits, disability insurance is entirely income insurance. The largest administrative costs come from trying to obtain medical information as to what the person's actual capabilities and limitations are. Doctors generally do not know what their patients do for a living, let alone have their job description or know what resources are available to that patient to help them do their job. Disability determination is a claims decision made in accordance with the terms of the policy. Insurers want an honest assessment of functional abilities. If the employee sits at home watching TV all day and their job is a sit down job, it is fairly likely they can do their job. Physicians are reluctant to say anything, however unintentional, that facilitates delays, fraud and abuse. This makes employee benefits more expensive and our companies either less competitive or less generous. Let's be honest - Having worked with Delphi Automotive, a GM subsidiary and spin-off, disability and WC were the biggest factors in their ability to be competitive, far exceeding the costs of their gold-plated healthcare plan. We know both WC and disability claims go up in hard economic times, especially when employees are afraid of being laid off. WC is a mandatory expense; abuse limits company profits. Overutilization makes it hard for good employers to offer good benefits, such as disability insurance.

There is more to be said about how to effectively work with insurers than can possibly be written in a single chapter, but hopefully this gives you some insight into the process.

Chapter 12

Government—Help or Hurt?

Government's role is to do what individuals, companies and states alone cannot do for themselves.

At this point in time, no country has done the methodical research necessary to responsibly take on the obligation of universal health coverage in the public sector. While other countries do not have the per person expenditures we do, they suffer from the same demographic issues and medical inflation issues. Our nearest competitor in the cost race is Switzerland with costs 30% less than ours.[163] Given that healthcare funding is the largest spending item for most regional governments in Europe, the rising cost of care is now beginning to affect their credit ratings.[164]

The United States is in the unique position as a hegemon, to lead

---

[163] This information was derived from the World Health Report 2001 – Statistical Annex. World Health Organization, 2001; page 164-5.
http://www.who.int/whr/2001/en/whr01_annex_en.pdf
[164] Skorecki A. *Health care costs hit public sector ratings*. Financial Times; March 11, 2004. Pg. 27.
http://search.ft.com/ftArticle?queryText=%22+health+care+costs+hit+public+sector%22&id=040310003931&ct=0&nclick_check=1

the charge to healthcare reform by leading the research. We have the bully pulpit of having the largest costs and the willingness to pick up the gauntlet and do the hard work of good, methodical research. We need to attack each catastrophic disease and determine what the first year costs are in each First World country. We need to seek out what elements make one country more efficient.

The government cannot afford to be complacent or slipshod in this research. We should be working with the ministries of health [MOHs] of other First World countries to coordinate the research standards for groups working on each disease around the world.

Our government can facilitate this process by giving first priority in medical research to funding the comparative cost analysis research. At least 65% of government funds for medical research must go to this area until we have determined who has "found health" for their people. As the leader, the government must keep the multinational panel of academics, clinicians, insurers, corporate and government researchers on task, using uniform methods.

Public policy

Congress has the obligation to write and pass good, well thought-out laws to assist this process. In the past, it seems the rush to get something, anything through Congress, just to say that they have done something, has led to costly, poorly written laws, the administration of which is left for bureaucrats in government to figure out. It is grossly unfair to these civil servants, as well as the American people.

Evidence of this is the Health Insurance Portability and

Accountability Act (HIPAA) Title II: Security and Privacy Rules, enacted in 2003 to supposedly provide administrative simplification and protect medical privacy. This law has cost $40 billion[165] to implement, by one estimate. After six years of tremendous inconvenience for patients, doctors, hospitals and insurers, only **four cases**[166] have been prosecuted as of July 2008. These would have been prosecutable under medical confidentiality laws already in place. HIPAA has grossly added to the administrative burden on patients, providers and insurers.

Under the guise of medical privacy, the law has done more to hold up treatment for patients in emergency and nonemergency situations than any other issue. Medical office staffs hide behind it for various reasons, when they don't want to give medical information to insurers. This even occurs when a utilization review nurse is trying to get the needed additional information to pre-certify a procedure for an insured; this is despite the fact that the payor has a right to know for what they are being asked to pay.

Fear of stiff fines has led many medical offices to clam up entirely. Confusion over who is not a covered entity has increased the costs of administering other benefits plans that are not covered under HIPAA, such as workers' compensation, disability and life insurers.

---

[165]*Assessing HIPAA: How Federal Medical Record Privacy Regulations Can Be Improved.* Prepared Witness Testimony, The US House Committee on Energy and Commerce, Subcommittee on Health; By Mr. Bob Heird, Senior Vice President, Anthem BlueCross BlueShield; March 22, 2001.
http://republicans.energycommerce.house.gov/107/hearings/03222001Hearing134/Heird183.htm
[166] Sorrel, AL. *Criminal HIPAA case targets employee, not clinic, for breach.* American Medical News, July 14, 2008. http://www.ama-assn.org/amednews/2008/07/14/gvsb0714.htm [Last accessed 6/8/09]

At one time, the Department of Health and Human Services listed clearly who was and was not a covered entity. Now it only lists who *is* a covered entity.[167] When an insurer calls them, most offices default to the "no cooperation" mode. Despite having signed releases built into the policy to administer the benefit, medical offices and facilities try to grandstand. This means multiple phone calls and faxes by the claims analyst/examiner or nurse, to get in touch with the insured for another signed release and, if still necessary, have the insured call his doctor. As a last resort, the insurer may even have to call the state medical board, because doctors have an obligation to comply with a valid signed release. This only leads to more hard feelings. Some companies try not to interrupt benefits because of this, but that leads to higher benefits costs for individuals and employer groups. Other companies cut off benefits immediately when they get no cooperation, which is unnecessarily hard on the insured.

In addition, the law has also impacted medical research, which is supposed to be exempt from HIPAA. It has confused patients, decreased patient participation, delayed obtaining information and increased the costs of doing health research.[168, 169, 170]

---

[167] DHHS' HIPAA Web site: http://www.hhs.gov/ocr/privacy/hipaa/faq/permitted/index.html
[168] Armstrong D, Kline-Rogers E, Jani SM, Goldman EB, Fang J, Mukherjee D, Nallamothu BK, Eagle KA. *Potential Impact of the HIPAA Privacy Rule on Data Collection in a Registry of Patients With Acute Coronary Syndrome.* Arch Intern Med, May 2005; 165: 1125 - 1129. http://archinte.ama-assn.org/cgi/reprint/165/10/1125?maxtoshow=&HITS=10&hits=10&RESULTFORMAT=&fulltext=Hipaa&searchid=1&FIRSTINDEX=0&resourcetype=HWCIT
[169] Ness RB, for the Joint Policy Committee, Societies of Epidemiology. *Influence of the HIPAA Privacy Rule on Health Research.* JAMA, November 14, 2007; 298: 2164 – 2170. http://jama.ama-assn.org/cgi/reprint/298/18/2164?maxtoshow=&HITS=10&hits=10&RESULTFORMAT=&fulltext=Hipaa&searchid=1&FIRSTINDEX=0&resourcetype=HWCIT

HIPAA is a prime example of good intentions gone awry; this is why *we need good, well-written public policy from Congress or <u>none</u> <u>at</u> <u>all</u>.*

Clearing away the bottlenecks

The government has an obligation to facilitate healthcare. One key area that needs to be addressed is the facilities to train the next generation of doctors. Our country's projected need is at least a 30% increase[171] in physicians due to the changing demographics. Our medical schools have responded by increasing class sizes, building branch campuses and building whole new schools. Yet, there is still a problem. Graduate Medical Education (GME), that is, residency training, has been funded by the Centers for Medicare and Medicaid Services (CMS), since Medicare was created in 1965. This is to compensate the hospital for the expense of training young physicians.

> Hospitals that train residents incur real and significant costs beyond those customarily associated with providing patient care. The Medicare program makes explicit payments to teaching hospitals for a portion of these added costs through direct graduate medical education (DGME) payments.
>
> …The DGME payment compensates teaching hospitals for "Medicare's share" of the costs directly related to the training of residents. Medicare does not make payments related to the clinical education of medical students. The added direct costs of GME

[170] Gostin LO, Nass, S. *Reforming the HIPAA Privacy Rule: Safeguarding Privacy and Promoting Research.* JAMA, 2009; 301(13):1373-1375. http://jama.ama-assn.org/cgi/content/full/301/13/1373
[171] *Addressing Healthcare Workforce Issues for the Future.* American Association of Medical Colleges. February 12, 2008. http://www.aamc.org/advocacy/library/workforce/testimony/2008/021208.pdf

incurred by teaching hospitals include: stipends and fringe benefits of residents; salaries and fringe benefits of faculty who supervise the residents; other direct costs; and allocated institutional overhead costs, such as maintenance and electricity. Other direct costs include, for example, the cost of clerical personnel who work exclusively in the GME administrative office.[172]

Medicare is the largest single program providing explicit support for graduate medical education…The amount of the Medicare payment is related to the share of a hospital's inpatients who are Medicare beneficiaries. All Medicare payments for DGME are paid directly to hospitals that train residents; none are made to the residents themselves. Medicaid also pays hospitals for GME in some states, but that topic is outside the scope of this brochure.

…Congress passed a law in 1997 that imposes a hospital-specific limit on the number of residents that Medicare will pay for. In general, the limit is based on the number of residents that a hospital trained in 1996.[173]

At present, there is no way to increase the number of paid residency slots unless Congress changes the 1997 law. Unless they move quickly, we will have young physicians graduating with no place to train. Without at least one year of GME, they cannot get a license to work; but unless they have completed a residency, they cannot get malpractice insurance or hospital privileges. In addition, the population suffers unnecessarily by having a lack of qualified medical providers to treat them.

The financial return on investment to the country has been proven. An economic impact study completed in 2007 by The Robert Graham Center for Policy Studies, a research group sponsored by the American Academy of Family Physicians, focused solely on the

---

[172] *Medicare Direct Graduate Medical Education (DGME) Payments.* American Association of Medical Colleges' Web site http://www.aamc.org/advocacy/library/gme/gme0001.htm
[173] Medicare Payments for Graduate Medical Education, American Association of Medical Colleges, 2006.
http://www.uth.tmc.edu/med/administration/gme/pdf_files/medicare_payments_gme.pdf

impact of family practice physicians in each of the 50 states. It found that individual family physicians had an annual economic impact in their communities of $949,269 per year, in a state like Indiana.[174] "Family physicians provide employment, purchase goods and services…These figures do not account for a family physician's contribution to the generation of income for other local health care organizations such as hospitals and nursing homes."[175] Congress should be clearing the path for Americans to have the highest quality medical care available, rather than allowing obstructions to remain.

Another obstruction to providing care for our elderly is the current physician payment formula, also know as the sustainable growth rate (SGR), under the Medicare plan. This formula has decreased physician pay, nearly every year since 2002, which is the current base year for the formula. Annually, the American Medical Association and the American Osteopathic Association beg and plead with Congress, which eventually passes a bill with some sort of "patch" for the formula. Lest you think it an insignificant amount, on January 1, 2010, a 21% cut is set to occur. What business can sustain that type of cut? There are employees to pay, technology to upgrade and overhead to cover.

According to an article in *American Medical News* in March 2009:

> Establishing a new baseline this year would reverse that cut, effectively accounting fully for the interventions that lawmakers

[174] *Economic Impact of Family Physicians in Indiana.* AAFP Government Relations, June 2007 American Academy of Family Practitioners Web site http://www.aafp.org/online/etc/medialib/aafp_org/documents/policy/state/econimpact/ind.Par.0001.File.tmp/Indiana.pdf
[175] Ibid.

have made since 2002. The concept of re-basing received a boost in late February from President Obama... Even if Congress followed Obama's lead by re-basing the SGR, it still would need to repeal or reform the system through new legislation.

...Jeffrey P. Harris, MD, president of the American College of Physicians, also testified at the House hearing. He said masking the costs of stopping the pay cuts does not make the costs go away—it simply postpones them, making the true cost of the next patch even greater. "This creates an insurmountable barrier to a long-term solution," Dr. Harris said. "President Obama's budget is a marked departure from past practices because it acknowledges what we all know to be true, which is that preventing pay cuts to doctors will require that Medicare baseline spending be increased accordingly."

The American College of Surgeons also supports a payment overhaul, said John T. Preskitt, MD, ...testifying before the House committee. "Medicare payments for many surgical procedures have been reduced significantly over the past 20 years, and in some cases, they have been cut by more than half from reimbursement levels in the late 1980s, *before* adjusting for inflation."

... Physicians project a crisis in patient access if Medicare physician payments fall further behind practice cost increases. In a February 2008 AMA survey, 60% of responding physicians said they would limit the number of new Medicare patients they treat if the pay cut scheduled for July 2008 went through. More than half said they would not be able to meet their practice payroll and would be forced to reduce office staff.

...Whether or not Congress decides to adjust its spending assumptions for Medicare physicians, lawmakers still would need to legislate a costly fix to the current system. The SGR formula and the decision by Congress not to reset it in recent years has created as much as a $300 billion gap over 10 years between what physicians are projected to be paid and how much their costs of providing care are expected to increase, according to the Congressional Budget Office.[176]

It is time to stop patching; Congress needs to repave the road.

Enough time has been wasted in the last seven years on hearings and

---

[176] Silva, Chris. *Organized medicine pushes Congress for clean slate on Medicare payment formula.* American Medical News Posted March 30, 2009. http://www.ama-assn.org/amednews/2009/03/30/gvl10330.htm [Last accessed 6/9/09]

lobbying. It is time to buckle down and fix the problem. Let us get the formula right, so our elderly will have doctors who can keep their offices open to care for them.

These are just two examples of bottlenecks, but I am sure you can see the impact on physician availability.

Getting the benefits we deserve

A dear friend of the family became quite disabled due to a number of health problems. In addition, she was a widow a bit down on her luck. It was amazing to me how challenging it was to access public assistance in general, let alone determine who had what program for which she might have been eligible even in the broadest terms. While federal and state agencies are listed in the blue pages of the telephone book, the average citizen does not know which agencies offer even the most common assistance programs. I have since moved to other states and found it no easier to look these up elsewhere. Not everyone has Internet access and certainly not everyone who does would know how to effectively do a search. For example, how would anyone know that funds are available to help low-income grandparents in Ohio defer the costs of caring for their grandchildren?[177]

Apparently our friend is not alone; *One in four of the uninsured are eligible for public assistance but not enrolled—that's 12 million people.*[178] According to the National Institute for Health Care

---

[177] State of Ohio Department on Aging Web site
http://aging.ohio.gov/news/agingconnection/2008august/dn.asp
[178] Understanding the Uninsured: Tailoring Policy Solutions for Different Subpopulations. National Institute for Health Care Management Foundation Brief, April 2008.

Management:

About 12 million people (half of whom are children) are reachable by Medicaid and the State Children's Health Insurance Program (SCHIP) but fail to enroll because they are not aware these programs exist, do not know how to enroll, and fear being linked with a publicly financed program. It can also be difficult for them to *stay* enrolled.

Childless adults comprise more than half of the uninsured, yet there is little public assistance available for those who need help. Since 2001, states have been allowed to expand coverage to childless adults and others who have been traditionally ineligible for Medicaid. However, only seven states currently have such coverage (AZ, ID, IN, MI, NM, OR, and UT), and these programs often have low enrollment caps, cost-sharing requirements, or other eligibility limitations. "The paucity of public coverage for low-income childless adults is really troubling. This is a population that really can only be helped by an expansion of public programs or some form of subsidy, yet we don't see a lot of that out there across the states," says Nancy Chockley, president and CEO of NIHCM Foundation...Since public program eligibility is more restrictive for adults, only 29 percent of uninsured parents (3.6 million) and 10 percent of uninsured childless adults (2.4 million) are reachable through public programs, the report says.

Administrative hassles can inhibit both enrollment and retention in these programs. New enrollees often are daunted by the paperwork required to enroll in a program, while existing enrollees can be involuntarily disenrolled if they do not complete renewal forms... states often make it more difficult to enroll when they run into funding problems. Chockley acknowledges that current state budget shortfalls not only make it less likely that states will be able to increase enrollment among people who are currently eligible, but also dampen the outlook for expanding eligibility to others. Massachusetts offers a lesson. Demand for the subsidized insurance program under the state's new health reform law has greatly surpassed what was expected and the program is expected to double its size over the next three years. The result, says the NIHCM report: "This anticipated demand may force the state to cut back the program."[179]

We can solve a <u>quarter</u> of the health coverage problem by not making the process such a mystery and getting rid of the red tape. Would it not seem reasonable that we require telephone books to have a page before the government blue pages entitled, "Do you need assistance?" It would list public and charitable programs, brief eligibility requirements, the agency or nonprofit, a telephone number and Web site to learn more.

Our government—servant of the people

Congress is paid to write good, well-reasoned laws. By running for office, taking an oath and accepting a salary, our legislators have entered into a contractual relationship. We must hold them to those terms. We need leaders who will roll up their sleeves and do the homework required to understand the situation in its entirety, along with possible unintended consequences of policy.

We must work together to come to a fiscally viable solution, or we have already failed. ***It is better to do nothing than to make the situation worse by bad laws, because it will only <u>accelerate</u> the current catastrophic course.*** We must do our due diligence and "find health" for our system, for sick patients and the American people. We have the obligation to get it right.

Government must facilitate the process, rather than impede it.

---

[179] *One In Four Uninsured Eligible For Public Insurance But Not Enrolled, Says New NIHCM Report*, USA; April 25, 2008.
http://www.medicalnewstoday.com/articles/105328.php

This is hard, back-breaking, in the trenches work that must be done for the good of the country. No cutting corners, shoving it through and let the technocrats sort out the mess. The work must be done in an orderly manner. ***There is no politics about everyone having coverage for good, affordable medical care.***

Given that we do not yet know the real costs of care, we are in no position to publically underwrite universal care. We are, however, in a position to drastically streamline the administrative expenses of all benefits. This will translate to lower premiums and better benefits for the money. Who does not want a better benefits package? What company does not want to save money?

Taxing benefits
—Stealing from the rich or pick-pocketing the working class

Both political parties have proposed taxing benefits as a means of paying for those without benefits. The President says we must cut the cost of healthcare because it is making us less competitive in the world market, I agree; eventually it will.

We want everyone to have healthcare. We would like all companies and individuals to be able to purchase it at a reasonable price. Taxing benefits effectively reduces the income of employees working for a good company that is trying to be good to its employees. Don't we all want to work for "good companies" with "good benefits"? Why would anyone want to make it harder for employees to have good benefits? This is counterproductive. By taxing employee benefits, our citizens have less money in their pockets to spend on other goods and services, ultimately leading to further economic slowdown. We definitely need a better solution.

The myth of universal coverage abroad—No free lunch

Much has been made about universal coverage and our lack of it here in this country. This argument is usually made by people who have little or no familiarity working with other healthcare systems. Having lived and worked abroad, as well as having worked for a global health and travel insurer for the last two years, this issue must be addressed. In nearly every other country in the world, you had better show your health card or credit card, or doctors will turn you away, emergency or not. This is the only country I know of where anyone from anywhere who shows up at a hospital will get treatment.

Many mistakenly believe that with nationalized insurance, the care is "free" to all. A conceptual egalitarian utopia has been presented that *is just not reality*.

This is what Dr. Younger, a Canadian orthopedic surgeon, had to say in response to this notion:

> In his film "SiCKO," Michael Moore contends that Canadian health care is free: This is absolutely not the case. Canadians pay out of their own pockets for about 30 percent of their health care for items——such as physiotherapy, eye glasses, prosthetics, braces, dental care, podiatric care, and home help—that are often covered by insurance in other countries. They pay the other 70 percent through their taxes. As a Canadian taxpayer, I am upset that Mr. Moore or anyone else should call this "free" care. Furthermore, in many provinces, Canadian citizens have to pay an insurance premium of about $100 per month for the average family. Although this is a nominal amount, it means the system isn't "free." In

addition, in British Columbia, approximately 10 percent of residents fail to pay their premiums, which means that doctors must either deny care to them or provide the care for free.[180]

Let us also consider the French system.

French employers and their employees pay wage levies of approximately 20%; employers contribute 13% and workers 7%...In France, insurance premiums flow into one of several quasi-public insurance funds that are jointly administered by employer and employee representatives. ...Indeed, fully *84% of the population benefits from supplementary insurance coverage that pays all or part of the medical fees that are <u>uncovered</u> by their health insurance fund.* In 1996, these supplementary providers financed 12% of all health care expenditures while 13% of what Americans would term deductibles or co-payments was left to households.[181]

The patient has to present his card called *"Carte Vitale"* which transmits all transactions to the *caisse d' assurance* where he/she is registered. All medical procedures (hospitalization, laboratory tests, x-rays…) have to take place in the locality of his/her *caisse d'assurance*. However, the patient can buy medicines anywhere in France and have the reimbursement later deposited on his/her bank account, usually within a ten-day-period.

An average of 70 percent of the cost of a visit to a family doctor or specialist is refunded. Reimbursements are on average of: 95 percent for a major surgery, 80 percent for minor surgery, 95 to 100 percent for pregnancy and childbirth, 70 percent for x-rays, routine dental care and nursing care at home. Reimbursements for prescribed medicines depend on the type of medication and range from 15 percent to 65 percent.

The percentage that is to be paid by the patient and not reimbursed by the *Sécurité sociale* is called *ticket modérateur*. This fraction varies following each individual's obligatory regime set by the tariff

---

[180] Alastair S.E. Younger, MD, FRCS(S). *Health care in Canada: Different, but not necessarily better.* American Academy of Orthopedic Surgeons, August 2007. http://www.aaos.org/news/bulletin/aug07/youraaos3.asp
[181] Dutton, PV. *Healthcare in France and the United States: Learning from each other.* The Brookings Institution. http://www.brookings.edu/fp/cusf/analysis/dutton.pdf

references allocated to various medical treatments and associated fees encountered. A patient can receive 100 percent coverage under certain conditions, such as having a chronic or acute medical condition (including cancer, insulin-dependent <u>diabetes</u>, heart disease…), requiring long-term care, having a long-standing condition, requiring a hospital stay of more than 30 days.[182]

Note: French citizen must pay upfront the out-of-pocket costs for healthcare and prescriptions. This is true in most nationalized systems; they tend to be *reimbursement programs*. They do not eliminate the personal responsibility of the citizen patient. Bring your Visa card.

In Italy, 25% of the healthcare expenditures, including co-payments, are privately paid.[183]

Italy has two main types of out-of-pocket payments. The first is demand-side cost-sharing: a co-payment for diagnostic procedures, pharmaceuticals and specialist visits. The second is direct payment by users for the purchase of private health care services and over-the-counter drugs. Mapelli estimated that, in 1995, these two sources represented 27.2% of total health care expenditure and 91% of all private health care expenditure. The remaining 9% of private financing comprised mutual fund contributions and private insurance premiums.[184]

The exact role of the private insurance sector in Italy is not well known…in 1999, however, an estimated 30% of the population was covered by private insurance. This additional coverage allows enrollees to obtain services through private providers who are not

[182] Brunner, Stephanie. *The French Health Care System*. Medical News Today, June 8, 2009. http://www.medicalnewstoday.com/articles/9994.php
[183] *Highlights on Health in Italy.* World Health Organization, 2004. http://www.euro.who.int/document/E88550.pdf
[184] Donatini A, Rico A, D'Ambrosio MG, Lo Scalzo A, Orzella L, Cicchetti A, Profili S. *Health Care Systems in Transition – Italy 2001*. European Observatory on Healthcare Systems EUR/01/5012667 (ITA), page 46. http://www.euro.who.int/document/e73096.pdf

accredited by the NHS, which usually ensures easier, quicker access to the services and often more comfortable health care settings.[185]

Universal coverage does not mean that there are no co-pays or that 100% of all prescription drugs are covered. Contributions must still be paid, or there is no right to healthcare, even in the Belgian system, which rated the highest in customer satisfaction in Europe. No system is perfect; there are flaws in each. If people will not or cannot put up the money up-front, there may still be delays in care, if they do not have a credit card in hand. People choose how to spend their money. Personal responsibility is not eliminated.

Universal coverage does not eliminate the need for a supplemental private insurance program. In fact, private programs are a growing trend, as national plans shift rising costs on the public. Consider Denmark, which year over year has won the "happiest people" award.[186] It seems the happiest people on earth also pay some of the highest income tax rates on earth, between 50 to 70 percent; in return, the government spends more per capita on children and the elderly than any other country, covering all health and education needs.[187] But their ability to continue this level of benefits appears to be changing. Now, one in five Danes has a supplemental private health policy, in addition to the public plan, with the greatest growth coming from retirees.[188] The average American would never tolerate that level

---

[185] Ibid, Page 35.

[186] *And The Happiest Place On Earth Is...Morley Safer on why the Danes are Considered the Happiest People on Earth.* CBS News, 60 Minutes; February 14, 2008. http://www.cbsnews.com/stories/2008/02/14/60minutes/main3833797.shtml

[187] Weir B, Johnson, S. *Denmark: The Happiest Place on Earth Despite High Taxes, Danes Rank Themselves as Happy and Content,* ABC News 20/20, January 8, 2007. http://abcnews.go.com/2020/story?id=4086092&page=1

[188] *Private health insurance on the rise.* The Copenhagen Post Online. June 16, 2009.

of taxation, let alone *still* have to pay for a supplemental health policy.

There may be a way to ensure nearly all are covered, but the current nationalized healthcare plans elsewhere would not work or be necessary in the United States. If we are considering any type of national plan, we need to set realistic expectations for our healthcare system. No nationalized system out there eliminates personal responsibility, including up-front co-pays. A few souls will escape any system. Visitors and immigrants, legal or illegal, are typically not covered, under nationalized plans, except under special circumstances. The global trend in nationalized systems is to shift costs to the private sector—patients and supplemental carriers. This would seem to indicate that inadequacies are beginning to emerge due to worldwide demographic shifts and rising medical costs. These would have been more noticeable elsewhere sooner had the next most expensive country not been operating at a 30% systemic discount to ours.

http://www.cphpost.dk/news/national/88-national/45964-private-health-insurance-on-the-rise.html

Chapter 13

Health for All—How do we get there?

No one wants to see people without healthcare benefits or bankrupted by medical expenses. Reuters reported a study recently stating that 60% of US personal bankruptcies are attributable to medical bills.[189] We all agree this should not happen.

We all agree that healthcare should be affordable. To do so, we need transparency and costs controlled. We also want to deliver the best care possible.

Political, rather than sound economic or clinical solutions, have been bandied about, causing much apprehension among the American people. A recent Gallup survey said that 70% of Americans were happy with their healthcare plans. Having worked for insurers over the years, one important thing I have learned from sales is that people are particular. They want the plan they want. Frankly, it would be far easier for insurers if that were not the case, but that is just not the reality of the industry.

One party has the "hope without a clue" plan, in which the

---

[189] Fox, Maggie. *Medical bills underlie 60 percent of U.S. bankrupts: study.* Reuters, June 4, 2009. http://www.reuters.com/article/newsOne/idUSTRE5530Y020090604

country takes a leap into the deep abyss hoping there is a big enough safety net, called preventive care, strong enough to at least slow us down as spending reaches terminal velocity. (If you have read this far, you know better.) Then there is the "no plan" party, which has yet to offer any credible alternatives.

When politicians admit to being too lazy to read the bills they pass, expecting them to come up with real solutions to any issue, let alone one as complex as healthcare, is illogical and perhaps even insane – if you believe the definition of insanity is doing the same thing over and over again expecting a different result.

As a humanitarian and patriotic American, I believe the country deserves a responsible solution to address this problem with solid answers and sound financials that will have a positive impact on both coverage options and healthcare delivery.

Treating the patient, not the symptoms

If we proceed in "finding health" by looking at who has already found it and what they are doing—we should be able to improve outcomes while cutting costs. We need to determine the *golden standard of care*, starting with the big-ticket items and then working our way backwards. If we do that, we should see a dramatic impact on healthcare costs and total health expenditures fairly quickly. Until we determine the *golden standard of care* and the costs to provide it, it is difficult, if not impossible, to definitively say how much that savings might be. But, if we do the work I've proposed, we would know for certain within the next three years. I suspect the savings will be considerable.

With the medical records reforms presented here, much of the waste, abuse and fraud would be eliminated or more easily detected. Waste, abuse and fraud alone account for more than 30% of our current medical costs. As you have seen, this can be done without huge expenditures for the health system.

The real question that remains then is how to solve the problem of the one-sixth of our population that is uninsured.

Dissecting the problem

There are approximately 46.5 million people without insurance coverage. In the previous chapter, we learned that one quarter, 12 million, of these people could be covered under current public plans. Approximately 16% (7.4 million) of the uninsured could afford to purchase healthcare on their own, as their incomes are more than four times the federal poverty level ($41,000 for individuals and $83,000 for a family of four).[190] Of those that could afford insurance, 75% are childless adults; the rest of the households are about equally divided between parents and children.[191] The fact that they choose not to spend their money on that purchase is a personal decision. (Yes, there may be other reasons, but stick with me as we walk through this minefield. We will get to them.)

---

[190] *Understanding the Uninsured: Tailoring Policy Solutions for Different Subpopulations.* NIHCM Foundation Issue Brief, April 2008. National Institute for Health Care Management http://nihcm.org/pdf/NIHCM-Uninsured-Final.pdf
[191] Ibid.

Another 5.6 million are illegal immigrants.[192] This should not be a health systems issue. This is an immigration issue for the Department of Homeland Security to address, since that is part of the mission with which they are charged. Personally, I have cared for and tried to find resources for many of these folks. But, as a matter of public policy, it would be disastrous to cover them under our public system. Frankly, it would be an invitation for people around the world to pour across the borders for treatment and would bankrupt the country, which is hardly fair to our own citizens. Besides, is it morally and ethically proper for one government agency to plan for the failure of another government agency? Setting up a system to institutionalize it somehow seems wrong. It also seems that the agency tasked with dealing with immigration should pay the consequences for not doing its job, out of its budget. Accountability is almost an alien concept in this country, but perhaps this might be a measurable line item of how good a job is being done securing our borders. Dare I say it might even be incentive for improvement?

Some 4.4 million uninsured are visitors, students or permanent residents. As a matter of policy, students should be required to purchase a student health plan upon enrollment. Visa holders should be required to show proof of coverage upon entry and renewal. Our embassy Web sites should advise people planning a visit to purchase at least a travel insurance policy for their stay.

Thus far we have accounted for all but 17 million people. Who are these people?

---

[192] Ibid.

We know some are young people graduating from high school or college. They often take entry-level positions that may not offer benefits. A study of 1,000 Americans between 18 and 21 commissioned by Golden Rule Insurance, Co. recently found:

> Two-thirds of college-age Americans rank health insurance as important as salary in looking at jobs. Yet just as many have made no plans to obtain health insurance once they graduate from school this month…It's…a problem for health insurers in general, which need generally healthy young people to join their risk pools to help cover the costs of more costly members…Only 18 percent of those who opted to take the survey said they did not need coverage because they are in good health. But 69 percent said they are fuzzy on the details of their parents' plan. One in four said they don't even know when their coverage will end under their parents' plan…"Young adults recognize the importance of having health insurance coverage but are ill-prepared to make good decisions about it when they leave school," said Rich Collins, CEO of Golden Rule and president of United Healthcare's individual line of business.[193]

It seems we teach our children many things in health class that serve little or no practical use, such as the fact that cilia line the trachea. However, it would perhaps be more useful for them to know how to understand, compare and purchase benefits plans. It would also help young people sit down and have an adult discussion with their parents about when they will be on their own. Insurance laws differ considerably by state. Some states limit benefits to graduation from high school or college; others are more generous and allow children to

---

[193] Wall JK. *Health insurers failing to attract young people*. Indianapolis Business Journal, May 20, 2009.
http://news.ibj.com/ibjemg/ibjemails/2009_05_20_IBJHC_Standard/Articles/38085.htm?l=1&EGEmailID=1305&PublicationID=3&PublicationDesc=IBJ%20HEALTH%20CARE%20WEEKLY&EmailType=Standard

be covered under their parent's plan through age 30.

The other uninsured people are in low-income jobs without any benefits. They may work for small businesses without the resources to provide benefits packages to their employees. This is the most vulnerable group, because they are generally less educated, less wealthy and least able to pay for private coverage. They also tend to be childless, which exempts most of them from any public plans.

While the issue may not be as dire as it appears at first glance, a good 5% to 6% of our people are truly falling through the proverbial cracks. That is not acceptable either.

Getting U.S. all coverage

Reducing costs enough to increase the affordability of coverage should be possible with the steps that have been outlined thus far. Given that nationalized systems are trending towards privatization, it would seem prudent to use *extreme caution* in going in the other direction.

Let us explore how it might be done without raising taxes on the American people in these already hard economic times. The issue is getting everyone coverage. While another public program has been proposed, this is hardly responsible given that we cannot afford the programs to which we are already committed. The other key issue of offering a public program is that it must be underwritten correctly or it will lose money. Given that we do not have a ballpark idea of what costs are, and given that nationwide insurers in the private sector were operating on a 2.4 % margin last year, do we honestly believe the government can do it cheaper than the private sector? (Remember this is the same government that contracts our Priority and Express Mail service out to FedEx, even though they already have post offices in every zip code.) "In a recent statement to the Senate Finance Committee, Lewis Morris, chief counsel of the Office of Inspector General, Department of Health and Human Services (DHHS), said, 'Although we cannot measure the full extent of health care fraud in Medicare and Medicaid, everywhere we look we continue to find fraud in these programs.'"[194]

> Medicaid had an estimated improper-payment rate of 10.5%, or $18.6 billion, for the federal share of Medicaid expenditures—the highest rate of any federal program.

> Improper payments have been a "long standing, widespread, and significant problem" for the federal government, but Congress has not always been willing to appropriate the monies that the executive branch seeks for antifraud activities. In 4 of the past 5 years, Congress rejected Bush administration requests to provide an additional $579 million to combat health care fraud on the grounds that doing so would reduce budgets for curing cancer and combating obesity. Virtually no academic researchers study health care–related fraud activities, largely because—as Malcolm Sparrow, a Harvard professor of the practice of public management, testified recently—it "falls awkwardly between the traditional disciplines of health economics, health policy, crime control policy, anomaly detection and pattern recognition."

> In 2002, Congress did enact the Improper Payments Information Act to make these payments more visible by requiring executive-branch agencies to report on estimated amounts improperly paid and actions taken to reduce them…But, according to Kerry Weems, who was acting administrator of the Centers for Medicare and Medicaid

---

[194] Ingelhart JK. *Finding Money for Health Care Reform* — Rooting Out Waste, Fraud, and Abuse. New England Journal of Medicine. June 10, 2009.
http://content.nejm.org/cgi/content/full/NEJMp0904854

Services (CMS) at the end of the Bush administration, "the total amount of Medicare fraud is unknown."[195]

CMS pays third party administrators and insurers to pay claims, but there appears to be little attention to fighting fraud, as is done in the private sector. So rather than spend $580 million to combat fraud, we spend at least $29 billion in "improper payments."[196] By my calculations, that is another $28.5billion that could have gone to research, but did not.

Remember also that the more access to healthcare people have, the more they use it, up until the point it becomes inconvenient. So we must take into account that there will be more health services used by this group than prior to coverage.

Another key factor that seems to be forgotten in this talk about developing another public plan is that there is an art to underwriting claims. The first part involves predicting what medical inflation numbers will look like relative to contracts and discounts negotiated. But it is not all about numbers. There is an element of intuition or "fuzzy logic" involved in it. Those who are best at it tend to become vice presidents of large insurers. The risk assessment process involves getting all the hard evidence together and then taking a view about what the future will hold with any given employer group, given the average age, past claims history, etc. Government programs inject politicians and political objections into the premium setting process, clouding good judgment. (After all, we can always subsidize our proposal from the general tax revenues—or can we?)

---

[195] Ibid.
[196] Ibid. See graph.

Consider these facts:

1. If Medicare would have been underwritten correctly to begin with, we would not have the projected $86 trillion deficit. At the very least, the terms of the policy and premiums would look much different than they currently are. Is past performance a predictor of the future?

2. If a public plan is poorly underwritten, the premiums will be below cost. Since the private sector cannot subsidize these losses with money from the Treasury Department, in time, this will wipe out competition from the private sector. In fact, they will be incentivized to do so, because bureaucrats and politicians will want to claim they have provided a needed "service" to the American public. (To heck with the consequences, we will worry about those later.)

3. If underwritten correctly, how is a public plan any better than a private sector insurer offering a group plan with risk pooling? *It is not.* More attention is paid to such areas as disease management, utilization review and combating fraud in the private sector, and virtually none in the public sector. The government is not willing to pay for those services, which is why their administrative costs appear to be less.

4. Currently, the administration of public plans is contracted out to large private insurers, who act as the TPAs for the government,[197] who pays the bills. *Any talk that administrative costs will go down as part of a public program is utterly ludicrous. It will be the exact same people doing the administration!* The difference is, with a public plan, there will be less competition to keep those costs down, and eventually none. At that point, doctors and hospitals both become 100% "market takers." They must either take whatever the government decides they get paid or go out of

---

[197] For example, in Pennsylvania, Highmark Medicare Services, a subsidiary of Highmark BCBS, has the Medicare contract.

business. Remember there are $86 trillion in obligations for Medicare recipients alone. An easy way to cut costs is to cut provider payments, but it is not a good plan for sustainability. Hospitals may close. Doctors may emigrate.[198] *Where does this leave the American people? At this point, a true access to quality care problem <u>will</u> be created.* Only physicians' assistants and nurse practitioners will be left to fill the need. Where is the quality care we have grown to expect?

5. In general, the rule of thumb is that the incidence[199] of catastrophic claims is three to four per thousand people in any given year.

6. According to the 2007 U.S. Census Consumer Income Report issued in August 2008, the real median household income[200] is $50,233. That means literally half the households in America make more and half make less. Those homes headed by married couples have a median income of $72,785.

7. We want a reserve parachute for everyone. This includes not only the 50 million without coverage, but also the small business groups with 50 people or less for whom buying coverage becomes a serious strain should one of their

---

[198] There are physician shortages in every first world country right now.

[199] The incidence is the number of *new* cases of a disease or condition in a given year; this is different from prevalence, which is the *total* number of cases of individuals with a given disease or condition.

[200] "Household income is the sum of money income received in the calendar year by all household members 15 years old and over, including household members not related to the householder, people living alone, and other nonfamily household members. Included in the total are amounts reported separately for wage or salary income; net self-employment income; interest, dividends, or net rental or royalty income or income from estates and trusts; Social Security or Railroad Retirement income; Supplemental Security Income (SSI); public assistance or welfare payments; retirement, survivor, or disability pensions; and all other income. Since answers to income questions are frequently based on memory and not on records, many people tend to forget minor or sporadic sources of income and, therefore, underreport their income. Underreporting tends to be more pronounced for income sources that are not derived from earnings, such as public assistance, interest, dividends, and net rental income." US Census Bureau Web site http://quickfacts.census.gov/qfd/meta/long_IPE010207.htm [Last accessed 6/21/09] The mean income takes the total income earned divided by number of households, which means a few extremely high income earners could skew the numbers upward. The median income is much less likely to be skewed up, as it divides the population in half.

employees or employee's family members have a catastrophic illness.

8. We want our citizens to be responsible for their own health and we want to reward good behavior. To provide coverage, we need for those being covered to pay their fair share. Individual underwriting for this group of people will not get the job done. Group underwriting alone will artificially increase the costs to everyone without encouraging any individual responsibility.

9. Mandating health coverage will also inhibit companies from hiring at all if they have to provide full coverage for every employee, full or part-time. Mandating full coverage for employers who are not currently providing coverage will cause lay-offs or even cause them to shut their doors entirely. It will also put an unnecessarily high burden on start-up companies that will be the backbone of any economic recovery.

"Where do we go from here?"

There is a way to accomplish what we want without unduly forcing people to pay for services they either do not want or believe they need.

One way to do so would be to set up what I will call a Citizen's Plan (CP) Group Basic. This ***statutorily mandated, <u>privately- run</u> group plan*** would serve as the most basic plan of insurance. In the same way that the government mandates everyone carry a minimum amount of auto liability insurance, it is specifically <u>NOT</u> intended to cover everything. It only ensures that everyone will have some coverage after a certain level of costs in a given year. Hopefully, people will use it as a foundation on which to build. (See CPSup information to follow.) This plan would purposely have a very high deductible of, say $50,000 on an individual plan, with NO pre-existing conditions. (Don't be put off by the deductible; we will discuss how to cover it. Keep an open mind and stick close now. You will get *more* coverage for your money.) Under the CP Group Basic, all citizens (or their employers) would have to demonstrate that they have purchased a plan that is at least as good as the CP Group Basic coverage from a private insurer for both full *and* part-time employees. This means as a full-time employee, if you like your current plan, you can keep it. Employers must provide the minimum CP Group Basic coverage for part-timers.[201] Under the CP Group Basic, there are NO pre-existing conditions. Here is the rationale. With a high deductible, it should cost no more than about $50 or $60 per month even to hire a 64-year-old employee. As an employer, you must believe an employee is bringing in more than their pay plus $13 to $15 a week to your bottom line, or you will not hire him. Discrimination based on age will be effectively eliminated for small employer groups. Known or perceived health issues will also not deter small employers from hiring someone qualified for a position. This will allow the dental hygienist undergoing treatment for ovarian cancer to find a job,

---

[201] For part-time employees with more than one job, they may designate the funds the employer would have paid for the mandated CP Basic coverage to go towards paying for an employee chosen CPSup plan.

whereas it may have been impossible before, given what this would have done to the dental office's group "experience" rating.

You say - a $50,000 annual deductible is hardly utopia. I agree. It is not. The point is that a $392,000 liver transplant does not entirely wipe out some unfortunate, uninsured working soul and his family. *This is why there are also optional CP Group Supplemental (CPSup) policies for individuals to choose.*

When the CPSup plans are initiated or when a person changes from an employer that has a self-insured or fully insured plan, there would be NO pre-existing conditions, as long continuous coverage is maintained. Supplemental plan options should vary – from lowering the overall deductible to a combination of lowering the deductible and covering various services with varying co-payments or waivers of co-payments. One plan should mirror Medicaid options for those with lower income. I suspect about 15 to 20 different standardized plans may be made available to accommodate tastes, in the same way Medicare supplemental insurance plans are.

The optional plans are just that – If people choose not to participate, they do not have to do so. People do have the right to spend their money as they wish, whether or not you or I think they are wise. However, I do not believe in eternally penalizing one stupid mistake either. A person may upgrade to a more generous plan, but they will have a 2-year exclusion on the higher benefits for that pre-existing condition, from the point in time that they upgrade. The money spent for the excluded condition will count toward their CP deductible, but no payments for treatment of that condition or resulting conditions will be paid under the CPSup. If a person chooses to "go bare" with no CPSup and has a catastrophic claim, he may be subject to $100,000 of paid deductible and two years of additional premium. This is a significant amount of money and should be incentive for Americans to sign up for a plan that they can honestly afford. (Don't stop reading now.)

Lower income individuals (under 300% of the federal poverty level or $30,630), who are not eligible for Medicaid should be able to have a CPSup plan, equivalent to a Medicaid benefits plan, covered as an "advancible" tax credit.[202] This means that our lower income uninsured need not entirely fund their CPSup plan themselves upfront to get at least the coverage and co-pay levels of Medicaid; it reduces their total taxes owed in order to pay for their coverage. *It also means that the government does not have to pay the full costs of healthcare, as it would if it expanded Medicaid.* On the other hand, if people wanted a more generous plan, they would have a credit equivalent to the Medicaid plan. This gives lower income people choices.

For those earning $30,630 to $40,840 (300% to 399% of the federal poverty level), progressive financial responsibility is given to the individual, with diminishing tax credits. All credits should be eliminated after four times the poverty level or $40,840. For the self-employed earning over $40,840, health insurance would remain a deductible expense.

The question then is, "What is the employer's responsibility?" What about all of these good companies that have been giving their employees benefits all along? Will they be tempted to pay only for the

---

[202] Tax deductions reduce overall taxable income; the amount of tax savings depends on the tax rate. On the other hand, a *tax credit* reduces total taxes owed.

CP Group Basic plan? Small companies wishing to participate would be mandated to maintain their coverage levels in CPSup plans at or above those on July 1, 2009, with employees still paying their apportionment, so that employees are not short-changed. Given the large-group purchasing power, the CP Basic plus the CPSup Plans should give small employers and self-employed individuals more stability in insurance rates. Risk pooling will ensure they will not be hit with a catastrophic claim at some point in the future, which would wreak havoc on their group's experience rating. If a small company chooses to switch to the CP Plans at a later date, they *would* be subject to any *pre-existing* catastrophic conditions claims when underwriting and be <u>required</u> to purchase a 2-year rider to cover any *known* conditions or symptoms of conditions, whether or not previously diagnosed. (Note: This could be substantial, depending on the nature of those particular conditions. The reason for this rider is to protect the financial integrity of the Citizen's Group Plans and to mitigate switching to a Citizen's Group Plan immediately, when hit with a catastrophic claim. Companies must properly assess their risk tolerances, rather than abuse the system.)

This CP Group Basic plan ensures that employers who are not paying any benefits will pay something towards their employees' healthcare, rather than leaving them "bare." They may also provide a certain amount of additional money for health benefits and let the employee chose to pay the remainder to buy the CPSup plan they wish. Given the option of plans and the value represented, this would make it easier for employers to be better, if not really good, to their employees, despite the hard economic times. The bottom line is the financials of the benefits plan must work or the business will be out of business soon.

The CP Basic should cover one preventive exam annually. Initially, uninsured patients and small groups would have 10 weeks in which to sign up for the CP Basic policy and one (or none) of the CPSup plans. Failure to sign up for at least the CP Basic is tax finable. Patients will not suffer the wrath of pre-existing conditions if they maintain continuous coverage and have paid for a plan that adequately covers them. Eligibility for the CP plan is determined by employer size or self-employment. Since it is a national mandate that our citizens remain covered and demonstrate proof of coverage, the standard steps which need to be taken when leaving a job or after having been laid off should be outlined in the phone directory. This would help small companies that may not have a human resources department. The directory is logical because it also lists the brokers and insurers.

Incentive rebates on CPSup premiums would be awarded each year to patients who do not smoke during the year, who are height-weight, body mass index appropriate and who maintain good control on chronic diseases. Rebates should be shared between employers and employees proportionate to their contributions to encourage healthy behavior.

Ideally, we want many insurers in the marketplace, both for-profit and not-for-profit, to increase competition and efficiency. If we want to increase competition among insurers in an area, it would seem prudent to *nationalize the insurance regulations for health plans.*[203] This would greatly decrease compliance costs for insurers operating in multiple states, and *open up states to new carriers and more price competition.* State insurance regulators would remain responsible for enforcing those regulations for health plans in their respective states.

I do not recommend going about this process haphazardly. A private mandatory plan is a *major shift* in the marketplace and *unprecedented* in this country. It is not a matter to be taken lightly. This is a brief overview of what I believe is a practical approach to solving the problem of the uninsured and helping our companies to be better employers without taxing the productivity out of our country. *We cannot kill the geese laying the golden eggs.* Certainly various financial models must be run to verify feasibility. What was presented here was a plan for individuals. The numbers for families will vary by necessity. Although as earlier stated, it is the childless adult that tends to fall through the cracks. These numbers may be adjusted up or down accordingly, but they give the reader an idea of what might be done to prudently solve the problem without breaking the entrepreneurial spirit of the country.

Making it happen

Many solutions for reducing costs have been presented in this book. Establishing the CP plans; determining the golden standard of

---

[203] Some states have particularly onerous insurance regulations; other states, like Ohio, have regulations that are both protective of consumer citizens and fair to insurers, without being obstructive to doing business.

care; eliminating waste, fraud and abuse; and better educating our doctors, patients, hospitals, employers, pharmaceutical companies, device manufacturers, insurers and yes, even government, can all help to solve this problem. We cannot cut corners in how we go about this process. We must **all** do our due diligence – our homework! We must get it right, understanding fully the consequences of our actions.

The issue of fixing healthcare is a daunting challenge. This book lays the foundation for solving this problem. We have an $86 trillion dollar Medicare problem to address. We must have a path for the currently uninsured to get coverage, and we need to put a lid on costs for companies presently providing coverage for their employees. What is presented between these covers is not the diplomat's or politician's answer. As your doctor, I "gave it to you straight" America. As the American people and healthcare providers, you are now fully informed. The alternative options have been explained. What you choose to do is your decision. I am reminded of what Patrick Henry said, "We had better all hang together, or surely we will all hang separately." We all need to work together. Everyone must have their proverbial thinking caps "on" looking for ways to improve efficiencies in ourselves and others. Friendly, helpful suggestions and method sharing is all part of the process. This is an opportunity to lead the world in creating a solid, sustainable system. You now know where the minefields lie, and you have a clear map of a safe path through those fields.

I have visited, lived and worked in many countries. Many have been pleasant, but the one thing that was universally lacking was that uniquely American spirit. Yogi Berra said it best, "It ain't over til it's over." You might be the underdog, you might be down, but you are not out yet. Between two wars, natural disasters, a housing bubble and one financial crisis after another, Americans have been beat down in recent years. We need to tap into that American spirit that says even though it is the bottom of the ninth, with two outs and we're five runs behind, we can still come back and win the game. That attitude has made this country a leader. It has produced citizens that changed the world; we love to celebrate the Horatio Alger stories of achievement by individuals others would have given up on long ago. A "can do" culture has always been our most attractive feature. Ladies and gentlemen: It _is_ the bottom of the ninth, and there are two outs, and we are way behind…we do not have time to waste. With hard work and determination we can do it America, and with God's help, we will.

Acknowledgements

I would like to thank my editor, John Sprovieri, for his assistance in bringing this book to fruition. I am thankful for my family; they have molded me into the person I am today. I am especially thankful for my mother, who encouraged me to write this book. She is my hero, and should be a role model for women and mothers everywhere. I thank God for directing my path, even when I did not fully appreciate it at the time. And finally I am thankful for my alma mater, Villa Maria High School, where every morning prayer ended with the words of St. Francis, "It is better to light one candle than to curse the darkness." Let us endeavor to remember that each day.

About the Author

Dr. Smith has worked as a health financing consultant for the World Bank and a public health consultant for the United Nations High Commissioner for Refugees in the former Soviet republics of Georgia and South Ossetia respectively. She served as the Corporate Medical Director for Highmark Life & Casualty, a national employer stop-loss, disability, life, Medicare supplemental and a regional workers' compensation carrier. She was also the Regional Medical Director for Disability & Workers' Compensation for Delphi Automotive, a former General Motors subsidiary. Over the last two years, Dr. Smith worked as the Chief Medical Officer for International Medical Group, where she reengineered the medical evacuation process for her company's global health and travel customers, getting them to First World care in the most expedient manner possible.

Dr. Smith was the first to propose the formation of the Osteopathic International Alliance (OIA) in speeches she made at the American Osteopathic Association's (AOA) 1999 and 2000 national conventions (see *Journal of the American Osteopathic Association* reprints). From 2003 to 2007, she served on the founding Board of Directors. The OIA represents national professional organizations from 12 countries and 21 universities. On multiple occasions she has served as a Delegate for the AOA and the Global Health Council to the World Health Organization's Annual Assembly in Geneva, Switzerland. The past nine years, Dr. Smith has served on the AOA's Bureau of International Osteopathic Medical Education & Affairs, representing the profession before various agencies of the United Nations and other international organizations.

Dr. Smith received her Doctorate in Osteopathic Medicine from the Nova Southeastern University, College of Osteopathic Medicine in Ft. Lauderdale, FL. She has a Masters in Business Administration and a Masters of International Health Management from Thunderbird School of Global Management, and a Bachelor degree in International Economics from Youngstown State University. She served her residency in Public Health and General Preventive Medicine at the Emory University School of Medicine in Atlanta GA. She has trained at the Centers for Disease Control & Prevention and completed the summer program in Tropical Medicine and Public Health at the Johns Hopkins University, School of Hygiene and Public Health.

Dr. Smith is board-certified in Public Health & General Preventive Medicine, as well as Occupational Medicine. She is also certified by the American Board of Quality Assurance & Utilization Review Physicians. Dr. Smith is a fellow of the American Osteopathic College of Occupational & Preventive Medicine, the American College of Preventive Medicine and the American Institute for Healthcare Quality. She is an adjunct assistant professor at the University of North Texas Health Sciences Center, Texas College of Osteopathic Medicine.

www.ingramcontent.com/pod-product-compliance
Lightning Source LLC
Chambersburg PA
CBHW030923180526
45163CB00002B/442